Beginning Meditation After Trauma

Beginning Meditation After Trauma

A Path To A New Life

Dr. Sydnie Bryant, MSOM, AP

Table of Contents

If you are reading this book, you have experienced trauma at some point in your life and are hoping meditation will help you. I had a significant traumatic moment in my life. I found myself in a hospital room, waiting for another heart surgery, with no money, no job, two kids, and divorced. My ego and self-esteem were blasted into smithereens. My hope for the future was infinitesimal. How was I going to rebuild my life? How did I get here? What was going to happen to my kids if I died?

At this point, I was already a spiritually experienced person. I was a natural health professional with 30 years of experience helping people in trauma. I meditated, lived in love, and had crystals all around me. For me, I knew how I had gotten to this place in my life. I had quit listening to that voice in my head that had always guided me in the best direction. I let another person's voice be louder than my own for what I thought were good reasons. I was out of alignment with my true self, my inner being. Time to trust the universe, learn how to receive help, and get back in alignment. My happiness and health became more important than anything else. Meditation twice daily became my life raft. Lucky for me, I already had resources.

I was also so fragile that some types of meditation were too much. Most of the guided meditations were too strenuous for me, demanding energy I just didn't have. I needed to be gently nourished, calmed, and recentered. Aggressive breathing exercises were out.

Big visualizations of a positive future were beyond my beaten soul. My energy was scattered by the trauma and needed to be gently allowed to heal. I had done this 100 times for patients, now I was experiencing it for myself. In this book, I want to create a resource for anyone in trauma to heal through meditation.

Many people get focused on meditation due to a crisis. These calamities become the catalyst to allow us to meditate and take our physical, emotional, and spiritual health seriously. I discourage you from blaming yourself for your trauma. Today is no time for guilt, regret, doubts. Today is the time for healing and moving forward. You will express anger, shout, cry, heal, find love for yourself and others, and begin life anew. Meditation can be one powerful tool for moving onward.

I am sorry about the traumatic event you experienced; however, I am glad you have this book in your hand. The path to renewal after a traumatic experience is different for everyone. Meditation techniques are easy, free, and amazingly effective. A personal practice of meditation improves health, reduces stress, and creates clarity and calmness. Repeatedly I get feedback on a list of reasons why a person can't meditate. I want to help you get past that list, remove the self-limiting beliefs, and effectively put the love of meditation into your life. Efforts to be comfortable meditating are the most practical way to spend your time and energy. I know you will find a silver lining in your trauma. I know that your meditation practice will be one of the silver linings.

The trauma doesn't have to be recent to be worthy of your healing efforts. Childhood trauma, assault, betrayal, abuse, grief, loss, health issues, and more happen to each of us. Each person has the right to define trauma for themselves. What is significant trauma for one might be insignificant for another. Trauma may be the stumbling block to a successful meditation practice as trauma creates anxiety, restlessness, negativity, and depression. Sitting still with one's body and thoughts is difficult enough for most people to begin a meditation practice. When one feels the uncomfortable feelings of trauma, it is especially challenging.

I could easily say that we need meditation now, more than ever, post-pandemic. But truthfully, miscarriage happens every day. Rape happens every day. Cancer diagnosis happens every day. Divorce, car wrecks, death, and betrayal all happen every day. Indeed, some may say that being alive today is traumatic. Political, medical, and environmental stresses take a toll on our bodies, mind, and spirit. These meditations are designed to keep your mind focused on visualizations that connect you with your body, help you heal your body, mind, and spirit, and help you create a new life. Our goal is not to move on from trauma. Trauma is not something to get over, but we can get through it. Our goal is to weave the emotions into the new strong, beautiful you.

As we sit, we will lighten, align, smile, cry, be frustrated, and be proud. We will untangle the knots and through this process, you will gain comfort and expertise with an amazing tool for happiness. You will sit quietly, get in touch with your body, open to angels, fill your heart with love and begin to see yourself in a new life. Trust this process and know it as a steppingstone on your path to joy.

I use words like God, Goddess, Source, and Universal Love interchangeably. I see all of them as one. I do not wish to offend or alienate anyone. If God is your preferred word, replace all the other words with it. I will talk about angels, Chinese medicine, and metaphysical elements as I know them. I am speaking my truth with Light and Love. Embrace the spirit of the teachings and then make them your own at some point in concepts that align with you.

I have attended meditation retreats over a 30-year span with Zen Buddhists, Shambhala Buddhists, and Dr. Joe Dispenza, and studied many more. My style is an eclectic accumulation of all of them plus my own, and this book is designed for people struggling to make a meditation routine in their life. So many people think that meditating means sitting still not thinking for a long time. My meditations will keep you busy, mastering your breathing, body, imagination, and mind.

Read the instructions and then follow them to the best of your ability. If you vary a bit, don't fret. Embrace the spirit of the meditation. Each meditation includes explanations and additional techniques. The more you understand, the better the meditation. You may do them in order, progressing daily. And you may do them in any order you choose at your own pace. I designed this program to last 30 days. Maybe it will take you 50 or more days. That's ok.

I keep explanations focused and short. Many topics could be a chapter or a book unto themselves. I offer an introduction, a tool, and a way to apply the theory to your life today. When struggling with trauma, too much information is too much. We check out mentally and it may be easy to be overwhelmed. I don't want to overload the brain. I want to calm and center the whole person. I want to help you feel in control of your life. Simple meditations with simple explanations. Life is simple, life is good.

Do What You Can

You can only do what you can do. And that is enough.

I have been a Type A achiever in my life. Success was easy, and my life was good. I was an acupuncturist, businessperson, and mother, meditated and gave energy to my spiritual life. Five years ago, in a 3-month time span, I experienced divorce, moved to another state where I couldn't practice acupuncture, and had a heart attack. I had lost so much of how I identified myself and needed to rebuild step by step. Like the Type A go-getter I was, my expectations of myself were high, and my guilt and negative self-talk at the limited amount (in my mind) I was achieving was overwhelming.

The gift for me in all this is, first, that I learned that taking care of myself first was important. Before all of this, I prioritized my family, my patients, the business, and everyone else over my own needs. It wasn't that I didn't make time for myself. I just thought I was strong enough to power through the stress and overwork and would catch up later. I am a strong, capable, smart woman and was quite sure I could take on the world just fine. And I did, until I didn't. There was a limit, and I ignored the limit because I feared for my children and my relationship with them. And, I had eternal hope that all would get better. Then I found myself in a situation where it became necessary to take care of myself or die. Since that moment, my health and happiness have been my main concern, thus making meditation a priority every day. I know meditation is the best thing for my health and happiness each day. In the beginning, I hoped it would work for me and gave it my best effort. Today, I know the value of meditation because I have experienced it.

The second gift of my situation was my new mantra, "I did what I can do, and that is enough." I released guilt from my self-talk and lowered my near-perfect expectations of being the perfect earner, mother, and person in the world. I no longer accomplished everything every day. Something amazing happened. I took longer to make dinner and enjoyed cooking more. Walking became less about exercise and more about living and enjoying nature at the moment. The house wasn't as clean. Dinner at the table with my kids and family was the highlight of the evening. I encourage you to do what you can do, and that's enough. Processing your trauma is a thing you are doing all day, every day. No one sees it, there is nothing tangible to show for it, yet it takes energy and effort. Realize your limit and honor the process of taking care of yourself.

There was a relatively long period of time when I slept with a child plastered next to me on one side and a dog on the other. If I got out of bed, I would wake them up, and my day would begin; there would be no time for meditation. During this time, I had committed to 5 AM meditations. I needed to meditate without waking kids or pets to keep going in my commitment. Instead of feeling guilty about not rising and sitting in the "perfect meditation position", I put my headphones on, played my music, and meditated lying in bed in weird and wonderful configurations surrounded by children and dogs. I did what I could and gave it my best. Gradually, everything changed, and I was able to shift my meditation ritual. The point is, I didn't let this inelegant inconvenience become my excuse for no longer meditating. I did the best that I could do. I persisted, guilt-free. Persist guilt-free. Say that again, persist guilt-free.

While I am talking about eliminating guilt, I recommend eliminating the word "should" from your life. "Should" is heavy with guilt. Either you want to do something or need to do it. Those perspectives are enough.

The first two weeks of any new habit are the most difficult. Know that each day is an accomplishment to be celebrated. Resist the impulse to feel like you should be doing more than you are. Trauma impacts the "old you" and requires creating the "new you." Rebirthing. Giving birth to the new person who moves forward, incorporating the trauma into a new person who can laugh and live again. Rebirthing requires energy and time. Take it easy, take it slow, and feel accomplished just by showing up each day.

<u>To-Do List</u>

Smile at flowers
Sing
Try Something New
Pot a plant
Say Thank You
Laugh
Listen to your inner voice
Meditate

Energy and Vibrations

While meditating, you will begin to understand the importance of energy and vibrations. Get in touch with your spidey senses, your intuition, your angel voices, and the feeling of being around someone negative or positive. These are all examples of knowing energy and vibrations. For some, this language feels too alien, and I want you to begin to feel comfortable understanding energy.

These are exciting times in Quantum Physics and Metaphysics. Science once thought the atom was the smallest matter in existence and we couldn't go smaller. Then it was divided, and new understandings emerged. Science is now seeing that energy and vibration affect matter. In fact, energy and vibration come first and create matter.

As an acupuncturist, I love this. Qi, or simply put, vital energy force, is the foundational theory of our world and health. I understand how Qi feels in the body when healthy, blocked, or deficient. The ancient Chinese observed energy in their environment and correlated this to vitality in the body. Energy flow creates our world in traditional Chinese medicine and feng shui theory.

Let's add another consideration with homeopathic medicine. Homeopathy is a vibrational medicine where a physical element, like coffee, is then diluted and shaken repeatedly until liquid exists with no chemical elements of coffee still there. The coffee has been diluted to a vibrational medicine. Makes no sense in our current scientific understanding. Yet it works. Coffee in physical form creates nervousness. Coffee in vibrational form induces calm.

A Qigong teacher of mine once explained the test he passed to become a Qigong master. Using just his Qi, he was asked to change the flavor of a bottle of vinegar. His energy changed the vibration and taste of a liquid 3 feet in front of him.

Since the 1950s, science understood that molecule shape is how we smell. The shape of the molecule connected with a receptor, communicated with our brain and we associated a smell and memory with this reaction. Now quantum physics theorizes that really, we are listening with our noses. We are actually responding to the vibration of the molecules, not the physical element. We hear smells.

The point of these stories is the importance of vibration and energy. And the point is to begin to expand your understanding of our world, release some old teachings and embrace new ways of thinking. Dr. Joe Dispenza specializes in bringing science into meditation and is doing some exciting research. One of his quotes is "Change your energy, change your life".

As humans, we are made of energy and vibration. Everything in this world is energy and vibration first, matter second. As you begin to visualize and change your thinking patterns, you begin to change your vibration. As you consciously focus on your heart, love, and gratitude you are raising your vibration and aligning your energy. Each time you do this your body changes, and your life changes.

For me, trauma scatters your energy and knocks you out of sync. You know that feeling when you can't think clearly, keep stubbing your toe, and people react negatively to you. That is the feeling of scattered energy. Your vibration lowers. Then you get happy, fall in love and the whole world smiles at you. That is the feeling of aligned energy and higher vibration. No matter your circumstances in life, meditation can take you to a place of higher vibration and happiness.

After trauma, we often struggle to align our energy and raise our vibration due to the heaviness of our situation. It takes so much effort to get out of the ditch and sometimes it feels like that ditch goes on forever. The meditation techniques that I describe are practical tools to align our energy and increase our vibration to help us heal and get out of the ditch. Commitment and perseverance are necessary, but once you get a taste of pure connection you will become addicted to that feeling and do it again just to get that feeling back. The feeling of joy, power, love, and hope all wrapped up into one magical meditation moment is hard to resist.

"If every 8 yr. old in the world is taught meditation, we will eliminate violence from the world within one generation." - Dalai Lama

Trauma and Chinese Medicine

I want to offer you my natural health and Chinese medicine perspective on how trauma happens in our bodies. Sometimes this viewpoint exactly explains what is happening to a person. Finally, they understand why they have hair loss or constipation or whatever. Another paradigm of the body offers another explanation. When something can be explained, it isn't as scary and feels more manageable. Maybe this will help you, maybe not. I offer it with the hope of helping one person.

How Chinese Medicine Works

In Chinese medicine, health is the abundance and free flow of Qi and Blood. When Qi and Blood become blocked or deficient, we experience health challenges. Many things can cause our Qi to become blocked or deficient. Physical and emotional trauma may block our energy flow or deplete our organ channel systems to cause Qi and Blood deficiency. Other common root causes of pathology in Chinese medicine are poor diet, stress, and overwork. Looking at this list we can see how a person who experienced childhood abuse and is now a single mom working hard to provide for her family in a society largely ignoring her needs is tired, grumpy, overwhelmed, and quite possibly experiencing a painful body. I see meditation as one of the best tools to help this mom. Of course, winning the lotto feels like the best tool for her, and I hope she does. But even more than winning the lotto, changing their diet, getting acupuncture or massage, or taking supplements, I want her to align her energy through meditation. By becoming aligned, decisions may become easier and smarter, stress may be managed better, and smiles may shine brighter.

Chinese medicine includes the concept of Yin and Yang. Chinese medicine was developed by Taoists watching nature and humbly learning the ways of nature. Our bodies are part of nature and we must live in balance as nature must also continually find balance. Yin is what is moist, cool, feminine, nurturing, dark, and descending. Yang is upward-moving, warm, masculine, and active. An eggshell is Yang, and the egg inside is Yin. Crops in the field are Yang, once harvested they become Yin. Yin cannot exist without Yang and vice versa. When you look at the Yin/Yang symbol (aka the Taiji) we see each element contains a bit of the other. The black aspect symbolizes Yin and contains a small white circle symbolizing Yang as the white Yang also contains the black Yin. Within Yin, there is Yang, within Yang there is Yin. Yin and Yang only exist in relation to one another. Men aren't Yang and women aren't Yin. Each person contains both Yin and Yang and exhibits their own personal balance of Qi. Seeking health and happiness we must each find our own personal balance of Yin and Yang.

The Qi is flowing through channels and each channel has an organ name. If we talk about Kidney Qi, we are not talking about your kidneys as we know them in Western biology. Chinese medicine speaks of the Kidney Qi organ channel system. We have six Yin organ channel systems and six Yang organ channel systems. Each Yin organ channel is paired with a Yang organ channel. For example, Kidney Qi is paired with Bladder Qi. Organ channel systems have functions and descriptions that explain the human body. For example, Kidney Qi is associated with low back, knees, hair, and teeth. Each channel organ system has a flavor, time of year, color, emotion, and more associated with it. When we experience trauma, each of the organ channel systems is affected in different ways depending on you and the type of trauma. Following is a simple explanation of each organ channel as they may relate to trauma and emotions with a few suggestions to strengthen and balance each organ channel system.

Kidney Qi

What is Kidney Qi?

Kidney Qi is part of our constitution. We are born with a certain amount of Kidney Qi that we have inherited from our parents. When we lead a life that "burns the candle at both ends", that is a life that drains our Kidney Qi. Kidney Qi, in particular, displays a strong Yin and Yang element.

The emotion associated with Kidney Qi is fear. Fear is part of most all emotions. We may fear for our life, our money, our family, our health, happiness, or the future. The spiritual element associated with Kidney Qi is Zhi /Willpower. Do we have the will to keep going? Giving up, feeling totally depleted and without the strength to keep going, keep trying, and keep caring describes weakened Zhi and Kidney Qi.

Weakened Kidney Qi may manifest as hair loss, dental problems, low back pain, knee pain, general fatigue, dark circles under the eyes, or more. We naturally lose Kidney Qi as we age. Menopause may be described as Kidney Yin deficiency. What is moist and cooling becomes dry and hot, resulting in hot flashes. At the changing point of menopause, people must find a new balance in their health and may need support to do so. Trauma creates a changing point in your physical, emotional, and spiritual body requiring a new balance for your health.

How do you help Kidney Qi?

These meditations will benefit your Kidney Qi as Kidney Qi heals with quiet and stillness. Herbs, meditation, diet, quiet, sleep, Taiichi, Qigong, and yoga are all good tools for building lost Kidney Qi. It takes a long time to replenish depleted Kidney Qi so be patient with the results.

Liver Qi

What is Liver Qi?

Liver Qi is how we move and flow in life. As we get bound up with life's challenges, our flow is impeded resulting in negative emotions. Liver Qi is associated with depression, anger, stress, and irritability. PMS is a great example of stagnant Liver Qi. Just before her menses, a woman may feel snappy or depressed and her menses may have cramps, headaches, or irregular periods. Chinese herbs and acupuncture can greatly ease each of these symptoms.

The spirit associated with Liver Qi is Hun or Ethereal Soul. In Chinese medicine, the Hun is the part of our soul that survives after death. Flow and change are essential to our life. And movement is essential to the Hun and Liver Qi. An example of how Chinese medicine might work with the Hun is in childhood trauma. Possibly, childhood trauma may inhibit the flow of our Liver Qi and Hun. The person may become stuck in a particular place and time finding it hard to emotionally develop past that stage of their life. They may develop depression, like their parent, thinking it is genetic. Possibly, the depression is rooted in family pattern and not in the genes. Possibly, the cycle of trauma created a pattern of Liver Qi stasis resulting in depression and anger. So, I might incorporate physical and energetic movement into a protocol to help a person with childhood trauma and depression, freeing the Hun and soothing the Liver Qi.

On an emotional level, we need the movement of having plans, goals, ideas, sense of direction. Liver Qi is the organ channel system in charge of our ability to make decisions, and plans, and to begin to take action. A weak or stagnant Liver Qi person may have trouble making decisions, second-guessing themselves repeatedly. Or they may constantly make plans but never realize any of them.

Depression involving a weakened Kidney Qi may look like a person without enough "oomph" to care about life. With depression involving a stagnant Liver Qi we just don't know what to do. We have no sense of direction in life. Often our depression involves both Liver and Kidney Qi and manifests as "don't know, don't care".

How do you help Liver Qi?

As we described, Liver Qi loves movement. Walking, breathing exercises, and exercise in general, are vital for a healthy Liver Qi system. While Kidney Qi loves flowing regenerative exercises like Taichi or Yoga, Liver Qi loves walking, running, tennis, and more strenuous exercise. Acupuncture and herbs move Liver Qi extremely well. Visualizations of your future help you develop your sense of direction, creating your future. Alcohol helps move Liver Qi for a few hours, but there is a rebound action of increased stasis, worsening the health of your Liver Qi. Alcohol may feel good momentarily but be worse in the long run.

Heart Qi

What is Heart Qi?

In Chinese medicine, the Heart Qi is the emperor of the body, mind, and spirit. All trauma, whether it be grief (Lung Qi), depression/stress/anger (Liver Qi) or fear (Kidney Qi), or other emotions, are processed with the Heart Qi. All types of traumas or PTSD must include balancing our Heart Qi. The Heart Qi system is integral to all emotions as it houses the Shen. Shen is often translated as our spirit. A healthy Shen can be seen in the spirit of the eyes. Each emotion from each organ channel system works in tandem with the Shen.

Our Heart Qi oversees the health of all our emotions and is also the organ channel system associated with anxiety. Anxiety may present as tight chest or throat (the area around the heart) or racing heart. Quite often I describe anxiety as Qi getting stuck in the upper parts of our body and not able to descend past the diaphragm. The breathing exercise called Buddha Belly Breathing helps with this.

Trauma often causes us to protect our heart. Of course, we don't want to experience our trauma again so protecting our heart seems quite rational. Maybe your posture begins to show a bent forward tendency to physically protect your heart. Maybe you sit with your arms crossed a lot. Maybe you are hesitant to truly speak your truth with anyone. However, we must open our hearts again to experience the pure joy of a puppy, a sunset, another's love for you.

A balanced and integrated heart and mind are the tools for great decisions and life choices. The Heart Qi organ channel system is the Yin paired with the Yang of the Small Intestine organ channel system. The Small Intestine organ system is what separates the pure from the impure in our bodies. This function extends to the ability to choose who and what is good for you. Some folks are consistently entwined with situations that are not good for them. Everyone else can see it but they have trouble figuring this out. By working with Heart Qi and Small Intestine Qi we can ease anxiety, and gain clarity and peace of mind.

How do you help Heart Qi?

Meditation, visualization, journaling, acupuncture, herbs and breathing techniques are perfect tools for a healthy Heart Qi system in Chinese medicine. I have included specific meditations and a Qigong meditation for freeing the flow of the Heart Qi. Focusing on the heart in meditation, opening the heart in journaling and sharing, breathing into our heart balance and free our Heart Qi. The bitter flavor opens the heart. Dark chocolate and coffee are both bitter flavors and may explain why they make us feel good while consuming them.

Spleen Qi

What is Spleen Qi?

The Spleen Qi organ system is our digestion in Chinese medicine. Trauma quite often hinders healthy digestion. Maybe we have no desire to eat or want to overeat. Constipation, diarrhea, and GERD are common symptoms of weakened Spleen Qi due to stress and trauma. The emotion associated with Spleen Qi is overthinking. Overthinking is when your mind just keeps spinning on a topic and you can't seem to think about anything else. Insomnia due to weak Spleen Qi looks like the person who wakes up making lists or thinking about things to do. Because Spleen Qi is about digestion, it is also about nourishment. Maybe after a trauma, you have trouble accepting nourishment. You may not feel worthy of care, love, and beautiful things. When a person offers help, your open Heart Qi allows you to accept help and your healthy Spleen Qi knows you are worthy of gifts and love and can be nourished by them.

How do you help Spleen Qi?

Salads are not the perfect healthy diet for repairing your Spleen Qi. Soup and warm cooked foods benefit healthy digestion. Sometimes we need to spark a digestive fire. A bit of ginger, cardamom, and cinnamon in your diet helps you process your foods. Digestive enzymes may be called for, speak with your health care practitioner.

How you eat is just as important as what you eat in Chinese medicine. Eating slowly, with gratitude, joy and happy conversation is key to maintaining healthy digestion in Chinese medicine. Multi-tasking lunch at your desk or in the car is absolutely bad for healthy digestion and Spleen Qi in Chinese medicine.

Meditations and journaling focusing on self-worth and self-love help us nourish our Spleen Qi. Visualizing a happy future and feeling the experience of getting good things helps us root out any subconscious thoughts of unworthiness. We identify the subconscious patterns and replace them with an assured knowing of worthiness through meditation and journaling. When we know we are worthy, we accept nourishment.

"Drink your tea slowly and reverently, as if it is the axis on the world Earth revolves- slowly, evenly, without rushing towards the future." - *Thich Nhat Hanh*

Lung Qi

What is Lung Qi?

The Lung Qi organ system is the respiratory system and immune system in Chinese medicine. The emotion of Lung Qi is grief. We cry when we are sad. This association is fairly simple to see. I developed a 3-month cough after my father died. Childhood asthma has been associated with divorcing parents in some studies hinting at the connection between lung function and grief. Also, Lung Qi governs our skin. Dermatological complaints are quite common after grief and trauma though they may not present for 5-8 years after the trauma. I have treated several widows who develop eczema 5-8 years after the loss of their husbands. We grieve for losses and deaths. We also grieve for what never will be. Often when a person who experienced childhood abuse loses their parent, they don't grieve the parent as much as the finalized truth that they will never have a positive relationship with their parent. They grieve the childhood lost. A parent grieving miscarriage grieves the baby never held. When I help people with smoking cessation, we often find old grief that must be addressed to successfully stop smoking.

Lung Qi is the Yin channel, paired with the Large Intestine Qi Yang channel. Large Intestine Qi is about releasing, letting go, and controlling tendencies. Lung Qi is about grief and its paired organ channel system, the Large Intestine Qi, wants to control life so we never grieve again. To heal lung or large intestine issues in my Chinese medicine practice, we must work with both organ channel systems.

How do you help Lung Qi?

Breathing techniques as found in these meditations are perfect for helping Lung Qi. Getting air past the diaphragm and into the belly calms and balances. When we can control our breath, we may feel more in control of our life. When we can exhale slowly and calmly, we can begin to release control and flow with life. Acupuncture and herbs are again, extremely helpful for healthy Lung Qi as are journaling, visualizing, and creative expression.

Normally, trauma affects all these organ channel systems to varying degrees. If you have the resources, working with an acupuncturist comfortable with emotion and spirit level challenges gives you further insight and tools. Not all acupuncturists work on this level, interview the acupuncturist ahead of time to see if they are a good fit for you.

Just doing the meditations and recommendations in this book will go a long way to balancing your organ channel systems and developing an aligned and happy you.

WHAT SUPPLIES DO YOU NEED FOR MEDITATION?

You will create your meditation environment. Create a space that feels safe and inspiring by utilizing favorite scents and sounds. You are crafting a new habit of meditation. For now, do the same things every day. In a few days, I want your body and mind to say, "Yippee, s/he lit the incense; it's time to relax." The ritual of meditation triggers healing and relaxation. You create your routine by choosing your time, place, etc., that works in your life. Make it easy. Make it fun.

A TIME

I woke at 5 AM to meditate for years, and many teachers encouraged early mornings. The earth is quiet in the early mornings, and in our sleepy state, we are more receptive to deep relaxation. I encourage you to try early morning meditation at some point in your practice. I often hear resistance from folks about rising early to meditate. If early morning is difficult, find a time that works for you. 10 AM, 2 PM, right before bed, it doesn't really matter right now; just find a time that fits in your life, commit to this time, and begin. The destroyer of meditation practices is the phrase, "I will do it after…". Then you find yourself at the end of the day not accomplishing your meditation. Pick a time and stick to it best you can. Put it in your phone and set the alarm for your date with your Inner Being.

LENGTH OF TIME

We will start with short meditations of just 5 minutes. I prefer to slowly build confidence and familiarity and create more tangible benefits. Do the 5-minute meditations 3 times a day to generate more benefits. Gradually, we will build to longer meditations once a day while maintaining, if you like, 5-minute tuning meditations throughout the day. For me, now, I plan an hour out of my day to meditate. Sometimes I use all that time, sometimes less or sometimes more. My commitment is to prioritize meditation during this hour and allow space for it. When life stresses increase, I may meditate for five minutes two or three times daily. Happiness is my goal, and meditation is my go-to tool to maintain a positive state of mind.

"You should sit in meditation for twenty minutes every day - unless you are too busy; then you should sit for an hour." - Unknown Author

A PLACE

Anywhere is fine as long as you feel comfortable. Now, I can meditate while waiting to pick up my kids from school, in my bed, on my porch, or taking a walk. In the beginning, I used a particular space that felt separate from my life, a sacred spot to walk a blessed journey. Finding someplace where you won't be disturbed is essential. I have a rule with my kids about not bothering me while meditating unless someone is bleeding. My pets, however, don't care about my meditation if they are hungry or see me just sitting there not petting them. So, choose a spot, close a door, and take a bit of time for yourself.

AROMA

Smells stimulate our brain, sending signals and triggering reactions. Utilize only aromas that calm and center you. I love lighting a stick of incense to begin my meditation ritual. I use sand from my favorite beach (Siesta Key) in a bowl and put the incense into the sand. Each time I light the incense, I know my ritual of self-care has begun. Traditionally, lavender, sandalwood, or frankincense scents are calming. Essential oil diffusers or using essential oils on your wrists are also effective. Flowers and plants are handy for grounding us in addition to the quality air and beautiful scents they provide. A garden spot or a place in your house full of plant life is a great place to meditate.

I suggest high-quality products as many cheaper incense brands, candles, and essential oils contain toxic ingredients. In addition to the two leading multi-level essential oil companies, doTerra, and Young Living, I love Plant Therapy, Jade Bloom, Aura Cacia, and Mountain Rose but many quality essential oil companies are out there. Shoyeido is my favorite incense company and after many years of use I have never had a patient have a negative reaction to its use. All-natural candles from the cool vendor at the farmer's market are my favorite candles.

SOUND

Calming music helps at the beginning of meditation practice. Use headphones if you can. Find a piece that has no words and is designed for meditation and healing. Everyone has a favorite and an irritation. Some love flutes, and some hate flutes. Some love nature sounds, and some are bored by nature sounds. After so many years of practice, I have a hundred healing and meditation CDs. Most folks find stuff on Youtube, Spotify, or Pandora now. I will recommend trying something by Dean Evenson and the Liquid Mind series. Youtube has many good free choices when searching for "meditation music". Find two or three pieces you like and stick to them. Asking Alexa to "play meditation music" has thrown me with sounds I did not enjoy from time to time.

Binaural beats are quite popular for meditation, sleep, and relaxation today. Utilizing two different tones, one for the right ear and one for the left ear, the brain melds the two tones into one tone. The theory is certain tones help us go deeper into brain wave and meditative states.

A note about searching Youtube and other online sources of music, you will find a plentitude of guided meditation. Thousands of great teachers offer guided meditations leading you through a journey. Compare this luxury to the ancient monks who sat in silence and chanted developing their meditation skills. Which is better? Are guided meditations "cheating?" In my humble opinion, guided meditations are teaching skills, opening doors, and removing unconscious limitations. I liken it to learning to drive. When you first begin to drive, a driving instructor is next to you. You drive on your own at some point because of the skills you learned from that instructor. From time to time, you journey with a teacher, getting new tips, traveling on a new path, or just for fun. And then, you go back to driving yourself on your own, unique path. Because really, the fun is figuring out your journey on your own. You will find some of the meditations in this book online to help you. Choose them if you like but also, incorporate meditations without guidance. Driving without the instructor is different, but ultimately the goal in meditation.

POSITION

Keep your body as aligned as possible while also being comfortable. The traditional meditation pose is sitting up with a straight spine in lotus (criss-cross applesauce). I like a straight spine personally, but this position isn't always easy if you are coming out of physical trauma. Be relaxed and comfortable, but not too comfortable. Meaning we want you to meditate, not fall asleep. One good idea, especially for anxiety, is to sit in a straight-backed chair with your feet flat on the ground. I am short, so I need to move forward in the chair or use a footstool. If you choose your bed, make the position different from your sleep position.

If you find that falling asleep becomes a problem too often, find a new position to meditate. It is ok to fall asleep at the beginning of meditation practice. I believe that falling asleep is your body adjusting to your meditation practice. Allow it to happen for a few days and then make adjustments in position to encourage you to stay awake. One of the benefits of the meditations in this book is that we will keep you busy visualizing and breathing and not encouraging sleep.

CUSHION OR BENCH

Meditating on the floor and using a cushion or meditation bench are excellent options for meditation rituals and space. Cushions usually help with posture and comfort. A zafu is a round pillow that is placed on top of a zabuton mat. Meditation benches are helpful if you have trouble sitting in lotus posture. None of it is necessary for a great meditation but it might help you create your sacred space and get you excited about meditation. Let the choices come organically. To begin, keep it simple and easy. As you grow your confidence, play around with tools that may improve your experience.

SLEEP MASK / EYE MASK

A Dr. Joe Dispenza retreat encouraged me to try a mask to cover my eyes. I have to say I like it and encourage you to wear a mask. I find it helps me focus and relax. It also provides one more ritual step to let your body, mind, and soul know that it is time to meditate. The mask also cues other people around me to leave me alone.

A TIMER

New meditators often keep one eye on the clock, wondering how much longer do they have to sit here! How long have I been doing this? Can I go now? For now, set a timer, so you don't have to wonder. Each meditation in this book suggests an appropriate length of time to sit in meditation. You will sit in meditation until the timer goes off.

Unease, anxiety, tension, stress, and worry are all forms of fear caused by too much future and insufficient presence. Guilt, regret, resentment, grievances, sadness, bitterness, and all forms of unforgiveness are caused by too much past, and not enough presence. – Eckhart Tolle

PRESENCE

One of the goals of meditation is to be present and in
the moment. Just be who you are at this moment. All
feelings about the past are history. All worries about
the future are not necessary. Sit with yourself in all
your beautiful splendor.

PATIENCE

Meditation is both the easiest thing in the world and
the most difficult. The main factor that makes it
difficult is our mindset, self-talk, and expectations.
EVERY meditator has moments of drifting off,
wondering about lunch, phone calls, etc. Slipping in
and out of the meditative state is normal. Just take a
breath, and think, "now my time is for meditating," and
refocus. No worries. You may spend more time
refocusing than focusing at the beginning of your
practice. That's ok. Every day your meditations will
get better and more magical. Have patience and trust
the process. You are on a journey.

To paraphrase Abraham Hicks: If
you are traveling from Kansas to
California and hit the Rocky
Mountains, you aren't going to think
these huge rocks are in my way; this
didn't work, I'm going home. Patiently
go through the mountains and
continue your journey. I promise you,
that meditation is worth your effort.
Persevere.

Even the smallest step is progress.

"Never discourage anyone who continually makes
progress, no matter how slow." - Plato

Day 1

Celebrate the first step on the path!

Set your timer for 3 minutes

Positive Thoughts:

"I am on a healing path"

"I am proud of myself"

Begin your meditation in your new space after setting a peaceful scene. Close your eyes. Relax your body. Relax your shoulders. Place your hands on your belly, just below the belly button.

On your inhale, breath through your nose, making your belly big, and then exhale through your mouth. I call this the Buddha's belly breath, making your belly big like a Buddha's belly. Do this for three breaths.

To yourself, say, "I have begun." Now do another 3 Buddha belly breaths. To yourself, say, "I am on a healing path." Now do another 3 Buddha belly breaths.

As your mind wanders, it's ok. Repeat today's positive thoughts to yourself slowly until the timer goes off. Sit and be proud of yourself for this success.

Insights:

Often, trauma causes our energy to get stuck in the upper aspects of our body. In Chinese medicine, anxiety and grief live in the heart and lungs, the upper area of the torso. A tight chest, headaches, and short, shallow breathing are all common reactions to trauma. The diaphragm may go into spasm or feel tense, not allowing deep, calm, and efficient breathing. By breathing into the belly, past the diaphragm, we better utilize our lungs and begin to feel in control of our body and life. Don't worry if it doesn't feel comfortable in the beginning. With each exhale, let your breath go freely, a whole-body relaxation. You are letting go with exhale, surrendering. Keep practicing by doing Buddha belly breaths in sets of three anytime fear and anxiety start to take over.

"In ancient China, the Taoists taught that a constant inner smile, a smile to oneself, insured health, happiness, and longevity. Why? Smiling to yourself is like basking in love: you become your own best friend. Living with an inner smile is to live in harmony with yourself."   -
Mantak Chia

I was blessed to study with Qi Gong Master Li Jun Feng, who insisted that we keep a smile on our faces during our Qi Gong practice. By putting a smile on the outside, we encourage the inner smile. I ask that you meditate with a secret smile. The secret you are uncovering is how fabulous you are, how magical the world is, and how you are experiencing miracles and peace every day.

Day 2

Set your timer for 5 minutes

Positive Thoughts:

"I see myself happy"

"I am safe and joyful in my happy place"

Begin your meditation in your new space after setting a peaceful scene. Close your eyes. Do 3 Buddha belly breaths.

In your mind, create your happy place. Real or imagined, it doesn't matter. Create an environment that feeds your soul. Where is it? Mountains? Beach? Home? How does it smell? What do you hear? What are you doing? For example, see yourself reading a happy book and sipping tea in front of the fireplace on a snowy mountain. You feel calm, safe, and relaxed. Know your happy place and go there often.

Repeat today's positive thoughts "I see myself happy," "I am safe and joyful in my happy place," and relax in your happy place. As you wander in your thoughts, relax, and focus again on your happy place and your breath until the timer goes off.

Insights:

Trauma shakes our faith. We must begin to weave a new belief into our life. We hope to have faith that there is a reason for all the traumas. We need to have faith that life will be joyful again. Visualizing happiness is a step to having faith that you can and will be happy. Many find visualizing at all difficult after trauma. Many can't imagine what their happy place is for quite a while. Imagine a place that sounds safe and happy for you. Creating a happy place in our minds first allows it to be built in our real-life world. You see yourself safe, nourished, and worthy. Meditation has an aspect of manifesting, and we are beginning to access our abilities to create with this meditation.

"When I started counting my blessings, my whole life turned around." - Willie Nelson

Day 3

Set your timer for 5 minutes

Positive Thoughts:

"I am grateful"

"I am blessed"

Begin your meditation in your new space after setting a peaceful scene. Close your eyes. Do 3 Buddha belly breaths.

Begin walking down a flight of stairs in your mind's eye. Count the stairs as you walk… 15….14…13…. and so on to number 1.

At the bottom of the stairs is a window. As you pull back the curtain, see something you are grateful for. Think to yourself, "I am grateful for…". Feel the gratitude and love in your heart and body. Experience the feeling of gratitude. Allow the appreciation for this thing to be your only thought.

If you are compelled, allow the curtain to fall back into place. Open the curtain again and experience another wave of gratitude for something else.

Sit in silence and gratitude. When the timer goes off, place your hands over your heart. Place your hands over your eyes.

Insights:

Gratitude is the easiest way to create happiness and a new life. When we are focused on traumas and worries, we may forget about the blessings in our life. Everyone is blessed. We are not ignoring or dishonoring our trauma by acknowledging the good in our life. We are shifting the load from overwhelmed to thankful. Look around and make lists of all the fabulous blessings you are grateful for. I am thankful for the blue sky. I am grateful for the tree. I am grateful for the squirrel in the tree. I am grateful for my pillow. I am grateful for strawberries. Redefine yourself as a blessed person instead of a traumatized person. Each time you do this, you take a step forward, out of trauma and, into the unknown beautiful future.

"It is impossible to feel grateful and depressed in the same moment." –

Naomi Williams

Day 4

Set your timer for 5 minutes

Positive Thoughts:

"I acknowledge the need for change and have no fear"

Begin your meditation in your new space after setting a peaceful scene. Close your eyes. Do 3 Buddha belly breaths. Feel your body relax.

See a shaft of white light beaming from the heavens, surrounding your body. Feel in your heart the blessings in your life.

Visualize yourself on the beach. Your bare feet are in the sand. Waves gently roll in. Your feet and ankles get wet. The water is cool. The sun is warm. Gradually, your feet sink deeper into the sand. You are free to move yet anchored into this spot. Breathe in the ocean air. Feel the peace and stillness. Quiet your mind. If your mind wanders, repeat, "I have no fear."

Sit in silence and gratitude. When the timer goes off, place your hands over your heart. Place your hands over your eyes.

Insights:

Have you ever stood next to the water and noticed how your feet become covered with sand even though you haven't moved? When your feet are on the beach, the sand beneath you constantly moves, and your stance shifts. The ground underneath you is not solid. Yet you are upright, strong. Even when the world beneath you changes, you can adjust and not be knocked over.

Through meditation, we change. We can't help but change. We become calm and happy. We may explore some dark places of our souls from time to time. Our friends and family may think something is wrong. You may wonder what is going on and feel the need to be yourself again. The thing is, you started this journey because being your old self wasn't feeling good or good enough. Often people begin to sabotage the meditation process at this point, the point of going into the unknown. From this point, you make one of two choices: commit to a life exploring the strange, beautiful universe and your soul through meditation or give up and return to the familiar, safe, yet unsatisfactory life you know.

Some will say, "I tried meditation, but it didn't work for me, so I'm going to try blah-blah-blah now." First, pursuing meditation doesn't exclude blah-blah-blah. Second, my guess is bouncing around from this to that makes you feel like you are trying, but you aren't comfortable getting past this point with any technique. Trust that even though your world may shift, you are strong, good, and looking forward to beautiful new joys.

"Before you heal someone, ask him if he's willing to give up the things that made him sick." - Hippocrates

The Importance of Change

Making changes to your life sparks so many emotions. Some people embrace change, love change, and cannot wait for change. Others fear change, postpone change, and grieve over any change. Each perspective is correct. Every view is personal. Be aware of the emotions surrounding your new choices while weaving the new *You*.

New beginnings are also endings. In our heads, we can see that we want to end the traumatic state. If the trauma involves grief, are we no longer honoring the person we grieve? We don't want to forget them by moving on. They remain important in our life. If the trauma involves fear, how can we relax and trust again? We must protect ourselves and our loved ones. If the trauma involves abuse, we must protect the child within while struggling to grow. We must honor and validate our pain, struggles, and situations. We must let go of that which doesn't serve us anymore.

Never deny the reality of your past, but don't live there anymore either. Attend to language defining yourself as a victim. I moved from "my car accident" to "an accident I was in." I was no longer defined by that event in my past. I honor it, appreciate the gifts the experience gave me, and weave those experiences and talents into the fabulous person I am. To love me today, I love all the events that made me.

While life isn't perfect, we may be familiar with our current life and feel comfortable in it. If we change, we are moving into the unknown, uncomfortable. We must embrace the new and unknown. Believe and trust in yourself, your guardian angels, and higher powers. Have faith that life will create positive outcomes whenever you make positive changes. Create rituals of support and celebrate each victory.

"This is a wonderful day. I've never seen this one before." - Maya Angelou

Day 5

Set your timer for 5 minutes

Positive Thoughts:

"I am in control of my body"

"I am happy"

Begin your meditation in your new space after setting a peaceful scene. Close your eyes. Do 3 Buddha belly breaths. Visualize your happy place.

Breathe in through your nose for a count of two. Exhale through your nose for a count of four. Relax. Inhale for a count of three, exhale for a count of 6. Do this step three times. Still your mind. When inspired, practice this breathing technique followed by stillness again and again. Sit in stillness and gratitude until the timer goes off. When the timer goes off, place your hands over your heart. Place your hands over your eyes.

Insights:

By exhaling twice as long as you inhale, your central nervous system relaxes, and anxiety is decreased. Inhale for a count of 1, exhale for a count of 2, and so on. Decreasing anxiety increases happiness. You now have two breathing skills. By being in control of your breathing, you begin to control your body. Your mind is letting your body know who is in charge. This step is crucial. Simple breathing techniques may not seem like much, but breathing techniques are a rich, empowering tool for health and well-being. We have begun the process of your mind being in control of your life. We begin moving your body and mind from living on autopilot or in "fight or flight".

The body loves to go back to its comfort zones, even when that comfort zone is unhealthy. About 9% of the people who make New Year's resolutions feel they attained their goal. What happens? One of the most popular resolutions is to eat healthier. And then… you walk into the office, and there is a big tray of donuts. Your body says, "It's just one donut, and they taste so good!". At that moment, your body is in control of your life.

Another example is you resolve to meditate more. And then … "I will later, I'm just too busy". "I will later … I need to answer emails". "I will later … I want to nap". "I will later … I'm just not good at it". "I will later … I just don't understand what I am supposed to do". Every time you talk yourself out of meditating, your body resists the impulse to change and would like to maintain the status quo. The body enjoys what is familiar, even if the familiar isn't what is in your best interest.

Your body is like that old Uncle who lives in the past and doesn't want to change. Your mind is the young person full of hope, looking for a better life. The mind is ready to embrace the unknown inexperienced world. Your mind is ready to brave new worlds, looking for a new, better life. The old uncle (your body's brain) does not recognize the authority of the young person (your mind-brain). One of the purposes of meditation is to develop your mental strength and not be at the mercy of the body-brain. You can heal your body and change your life with your mind.

"Tension is who you think you should be. Relaxation is who you are."
- Chinese proverb

Negative Thoughts and How to Deal With Them

If negative thoughts begin taking over your brain, there are a few tricks to get control of them.

1. Think of thoughts as items on a conveyor belt. When a negative thought comes along, just put that thought back on the belt with a blessing and, "that doesn't serve me anymore." Then choose a positive view to take its place. Replace unwanted thoughts with wanted thoughts.

2. Fill the negative thought space with brain games. When the thoughts that aren't serving your present goals show up, think of something that makes you happy, for example, puppy. Puppy ends in "Y" so think of something happy that begins with "Y" like yellow. Yellow ends in "W", and so on.

3. I constantly contact my angels and guides, and they send me messages through numbers daily. Have you ever looked at the clock at 11:11 every day? Or repeatedly noticed a

number on license plates, in money transactions, or the time? Each number has a message for you from your guides. When my thoughts wander to negative thoughts, I repeat the number I am receiving that day and remind myself to align with that energy. If a number isn't showing up for you right away, use zero, the number of all possibilities.

4. Negative thoughts might have been helpful for you at one time. Meaning, "I must run and be scared" is a thought that served a purpose once but doesn't apply today. Give validation to your thoughts and let them go with "bless and release." Each time a thought that no longer serves you pops up, think "bless and release" and let them go.

5. Ponder the negative thought. Maybe there is a message in there you need to pay attention to. Sometimes quickly ignoring a negative thought and replacing it with a positive idea slows your healing. Differentiate between habitual negative self-talk and a healing experience trying to reach you. Ask yourself, "Am I familiar with this thought?", "Have I

learned what it needs to teach me?", "Is releasing this thought in my best interest?". Know yourself, accept yourself, love yourself, and encourage positive energy in your inner and outer worlds.

6. Negative thoughts may be actual voices from the people around you. These people may be your parents, authority figures, spouses, etc. I call them the "Negative Nellies" or Nellie for short. Getting Nellie's negative impressions and corresponding negative energy out of your head is difficult because they tend to be people you have trusted and opened to at some point in your life. One of the benefits of meditation is centering and protecting myself from a negative person I am bound to by circumstance. The stronger and more peaceful I am, the less their words and actions affect me. Create a bubble vision around you and let the words bounce off. Do not give them or their words energy by engaging in conversation, explanation, or dialogue beyond the most necessary facts. Do not participate in their world by giving it your energy. Your energy is solely devoted to creating your beautiful world for you. This energy

removal sometimes sends Nellie into a backlash spiral but let that be ok. You are not responsible for their choices. You are responsible for yours, and you are choosing a new life, a new way of being.

7. You are deliberately creating a new you every day. You are changing and making choices about how the new you think, act, eat, breathe, and walk. When you find yourself in old daydreams, patterns, or self-talk, then think, "that is the old me, the new me does this…" or "that was then, this is now." For example, a person has dinner with a fabulous person but has anxiety over what they might do, spill, or say. The person has a self-concept of being a klutz and is feeding the self-concept. Let us release the self-concept of the klutz and replace it with grace. See the dinner going gracefully. If spillage happens, let it happen with grace. Change the self-talk.

8. The old adage "What you resist, persists" is good to remember. Each time you beat yourself up for negative thoughts, they will return. Surround yourself with love and know this is part of the human experience. Use all

these techniques with firm, loving patience. Be kind to yourself. It takes persistence and patience to disentangle old subconscious programs. Every time you consciously change your thinking, you are a winner.

9. Rest. I find I fall into negative thoughts when I am tired. Take a nap, watch a happy movie, or fingerpaint with the kids. Do whatever you can to feed your body and soul.

Day 6

Set your timer for 5 minutes

Positive Thoughts:

"Please forgive me, I'm sorry, I love you, Thank You"

Begin your meditation in your new space after setting a peaceful scene. Close your eyes. Do 3 Buddha belly breaths. Visualize your happy place.

See yourself in your happy place and recite this prayer to yourself. "Please forgive me, I'm sorry, I love you, thank you." Say it slowly. Rearrange the order if that feels better. Keep repeating it 9 times.

Sit in stillness and gratitude until the timer goes off. When the timer goes off, place your hands over your heart. Place your hands over your eyes.

Insights:

The positive thoughts today are the ho'oponopono mantra or prayer. Many Polynesian cultures traditionally practice ho'oponopono, and today the prayer has many followers. I want you to say this mantra to yourself and practice forgiving and loving yourself. First, forgive, apologize, and love yourself. Say this to you. This is a meditation you may want to do for several days with alternating focus.

Also, say this prayer to people in your life. Maybe you need to ask forgiveness from someone in your life you have wronged. Let go of all excuses for why something happened. It doesn't matter. Say the mantra. Let go of all the guilt, shame, regret, and pain that you feel. Say the mantra to someone you have wronged.

Maybe you need to forgive and love someone in your life who has wronged you. Let go of the trauma long enough to say the mantra while holding a vision of this person. You cannot change them, fix them, or punish them right now. You can help yourself and your healing by loving them for just a minute. You don't need to be friends with them, ever say anything nice to them or even do anything nice for them. You do set a boundary eliminating this person and their actions from your life as best you can. You can also free yourself of the negative emotions weighing you down by reciting this mantra and meaning it.

In these meditations, this prayer is mainly about forgiving yourself. Even "victims" need to forgive themselves.

I was working with a crisis counseling service once and worked with a young woman ready to disfigure her face. At some level, she blamed herself for her trauma. She believed that by making herself ugly, she would never be raped again. She needed to forgive herself for her trauma.

The parent whose child committed suicide has tremendous guilt about what they should have done. For that parent, this prayer is perfect.

I take issue with many manifesting teachers who recite the "you create your own reality" thought that often blames someone for their situation. I believe this insight has merits and I believe that it also is dispensed too freely creating guilt, blame and separation. I didn't consciously create the "bad things" in my life. I see a gift in every "bad thing" that has ever happened to me, and maybe each bad thing was created to fulfill my lessons for this life. For those who have experienced serious trauma in life, I want to remove the impulse to beat themselves up thinking they caused or deserved their trauma.

Today, you will trust that your trauma will have a silver lining, and you can forgive and love yourself, releasing any guilt or sense of self-sabotage. Please forgive me, I'm sorry, I love you, Thank You.

"Compassion springs from the heart as pure,
refreshing water, healing the wounds of life."
- *Thich Nhat Hanh*

Day 7

Set your timer for 15 minutes

Positive Thoughts:

"I am strong"

"I walk into my future with my head held high"

Today's meditation is a walking meditation.

On a beautiful day, do a walking meditation.

Choose a happy place to walk, like a park, a street with little traffic, or your own yard.

Stand with feet shoulder-width apart.

Place your hands on your lower abdomen while you set your intention for a peaceful meditation creating happiness, health, and wealth.

Bend your knees slightly. Relax your body.

Take three deep breaths. Put a pleasant smile on your face.

Either keep your hands on your belly or let them dangle comfortably at your side. Begin ambling by first placing your right heel on the ground. Heel to toe, with feet straight, begin walking.

Look straight ahead or slightly down. Let your attention remain with your breath, the feeling of your feet on the ground, the sounds of your environment, and nature all around you.

Remain positive in your thoughts. Keep your attention on the present moment, the current place. Allow gratitude to arise. Walk as long as you like.

Walking meditations are fantastic for developing awareness and gratitude for the present moment, the now. As you walk, realize how fabulous you are. Realize how beautiful your future is. Walk with strength and self-love, releasing the past, embracing your future, and feeling present in the moment.

Breathe deeply. Smile. Love life in this moment.

As you finish, stand still, place your hands on your belly, and remember how strong and amazing you are.

Insights:

In the Chinese medicine explanations of this book, we talk about the need for movement. Movement creates healthy Liver Qi. Movement is necessary to move your emotions and life into your future. Movement with attention to the present moment, attention to what is around you at this exact moment in time is meditation. Walking meditations make us realize that meditation doesn't have to be some foreign new technique. Meditation can be as simple as taking a walk with a present, positive mind. If you cannot physically take a walk, figure out what movement you can do and do that with breathing, love and presence.

"Planting a seed, washing a dish and cutting grass are as eternal, as beautiful as writing a poem." - *Thich Nhat Hanh*

Day 8

Set your timer for 7 minutes

Positive Thoughts:

      "I am not alone"

      "I am loved"

Begin your meditation in your new space after setting a peaceful scene. Close your eyes. Do 3 Buddha belly breaths. Visualize your happy place.

Think to yourself or say out loud, "angels of love and light, be with me to offer blessings and guidance in my life." Inhale for a count of three, exhale for a count of 6.

Visualize white light surrounding your body. Visualize your angels next to you, offering their gifts of healing, protection, and guidance.

Sit in stillness and love. When the timer goes off, place your hands over your heart. Place your hands over your eyes.

Insights:

I believe in angels. I believe in guardian angels. I think we all have a guardian angel loving and caring for us. It is easy to feel alone and separated from our angels when you have gone through trauma. Believing that we are being watched over and cared for when something tragic happens in our life does not make sense. I don't know if I have the answer to this dilemma, but I know I have angels watching over me even with my tragedies. I trust in a bigger picture than my perception of my disasters.

Angels can be guardian angels, archangels, spirit guides, ancestors, loved ones who have passed. They work best when we consciously ask for their help and presence in our lives. Ask for angels in love and light to help and trust who you feel, think of, see. Trust they are there even if you don't feel them. Eventually, you will.

I want you to consciously connect with your angels. I have had folks tell me they don't believe or are the one person who doesn't have a guardian angel. Make me happy and try anyway. The more we connect with our angels, the stronger their presence in our lives. More accurately, the more we connect with the angels, the more aware of their existence we become. This meditation is about our shift in awareness, not their change of presence. If substituting God, goddess, spirit, etc., for the word angels feels better for you, please do so.

"Sometimes the only support system you have is yourself, the angels and the power of your vision."

- Dr. Sydnie Bryant

Angel Meditation

I often call in several angels to surround me during a meditation. Below is an example of how I call the Archangels to bless me with their gifts.

> *"Archangel Michael, please be with me now". Archangel Michael appears on my right side to bless me with protection, clearing away all negative beliefs and attachments. Archangel Michael is a source of strength and protection when I am fearful. I thank him.*

> *"Archangel Uriel, please be with me now". Archangel Uriel appears behind me, ready to help guide me in the right direction. Archangel Uriel helps me know and clear my path forward. I thank him.*

> *"Archangel Raphael, please be with me now". Archangel Raphael appears at my left, ready to bless my body and emotions with his healing green light. Archangel Raphael provides clarity for rebuilding my life. I thank him.*

> *"Archangel Gabriel, please be with me now". Archangel Gabriel appears at my front, ready to aid me in expressing my highest truth*

*Archangel Gabriel aids in my
commitment and achievement of my
goals. I thank them.*

*"Thank You, Angels, for your
guidance and blessings. I am grateful
and offer a gift of appreciation".*

At this point, I continue with my meditation
feeling the presence of the Archangels
around me.

Archangels Raphael, Michael, Uriel,
and Gabriel, are the primary Archangels
charged with protecting humanity. They
are the angels most commonly called on.
However, many archangels are ready and
willing to aid you in your path: Metatron,
Seraph, Sandalphon, and more. Besides
the Archangels, other angels, saints, gods,
goddesses, spirit guides, and ancestors
may all be called on to help you if you feel
the impulse to connect with them.

"Give yourself permission to focus on good feeling things." — Abraham Hicks

Day 9

Set your timer for 8 minutes

Positive Thoughts:

"I am blessed"

"I am happy"

"I am loved"

Begin your meditation in your new space after setting a peaceful scene. Close your eyes. Do 3 Buddha belly breaths. Inhale for 3 counts, exhale for 6 counts. Visualize your happy place. Feel your body relax.

Call in your angels, asking for and expressing gratitude for their blessing. See a shaft of white light beaming from the heavens, surrounding your body. Feel in your heart the blessings in your life.

If your mind wanders, visualize your happy place and stay there or count blessings, feeling gratitude in your heart.

Sit in stillness and gratitude. When the timer goes off, place your hands over your heart. Place your hands over your eyes.

Insights:

Today's meditation puts together all you have learned. Now, you are comfortable in your space and comfortable with your ability to meditate. You have learned to control and connect with breathing. You have a place in your mind that is peaceful. You can call in your angels and feel blessed. That's a lot! These are amazing skills for handling stressful life events. You are now comfortable with being present in your body and controlling your breath, skills that will serve you for the rest of your life. Take a moment to feel successful.

*"The secret to change is to focus all
of your energy, not on fighting the old,
but on building the new." – Socrates*

Chakras / Wheels/ Centers / Vortex…

For the next 8 days, we will focus on our body's chakras or energy centers.

Chakra is a Sanskrit word that means wheel or disc. Traditionally, seven main chakras can be felt but not seen by most people; however, other systems acknowledge more energy centers. Each center holds moving healing energy that relates to our body's healing. The vortexes are in the midline of the body in ascending order. They have a front and a back and have moving energy both up and down and in and out.

The first three chakras relate to survival in this body and this world. These three chakras can easily be damaged by trauma. Our ability to feel safe, know who we are, and have all our needs in life met, like ourselves, etc., are in these first three energy centers. The next involve opening your heart and speaking your heart's truth. The last two involve connecting with love and forces outside of our body.

By giving your attention to each individual chakra and to the flow of energy between them and surrounding your body, you can heal, energize, and recover. Chakra work isn't a one-time process. Daily attention to aligning your body and helping your energy grow and flow is a lifelong devotion.

Day 10

Set your timer for 8 minutes

Positive Thoughts:

"All my needs and wants are taken care of"

Begin your meditation in your new space after setting
a peaceful scene. Close your eyes. Do 3 Buddha
belly breaths. Inhale for 3 counts, exhale for 6 counts.
Feel your body relax. See a shaft of white light
beaming from the heavens, surrounding your body.
Feel in your heart the blessings in your life. Call in
your angels, asking for and expressing gratitude for
their blessing.

Visualize a point just above the pubic bone, below
your belly button. See a red ball of light glowing at this
spot. Allow the energy to grow as you think "all my
needs and wants are taken care of," "I am centered
and grounded," "I am perfect health," "I am perfect
wealth," "I am perfect joy."

Breathe in and out, staying focused on the root
chakra and your growing belly of red energy with love
and patience. "I am blessed." "I am grateful."

Sit in silence and gratitude. When the timer goes off,
place your hands over your heart. Place your hands
over your eyes.

Insights:

The Root chakra is our foundational energy. The foundation of our life is finances, housing, food, sexuality, and safety. Trauma shakes us off our foundation. Depending on your situation, your foundation can be wide open, draining all your energy, finances, and self-esteem. This situation requires you to visualize closing the chakra to create balance. Maybe the root chakra is blocked, closing you off to change, creating anxiety, or over-attachment to money and things. Then you need to visualize the flow through the chakra. Allow it to breathe and relax. Take your time with this meditation. You may need to be ok with minimal change and move on to the following meditation. That's ok; just keep coming back to this energy center and allow the energy to grow. If you have been through sexual trauma, this focus can be challenging. If memories come up, acknowledge them, then think, "that is behind me, today I am safe." Attach the memory to a balloon and let the balloon float away. Take your time and trust that your root chakra and life are just fine.

"What the caterpillar calls the end of the world, the master calls the butterfly."   *- Chinese proverb*

To become a butterfly, a caterpillar does more than wrap up in a cozy blanket cocoon and come out a butterfly. First, the caterpillar must break down completely, become goo, use small bits of itself called imaginal discs and complete the fragile metamorphosis. Once complete, a new being emerges, a new set of behaviors, and ways of moving, eating, and living in this world.

Day 11

Set your timer for 8 minutes

Positive Thoughts:

"I am safe and cared for"

Begin your meditation in your new space after setting a peaceful scene. Close your eyes. Do 3 Buddha belly breaths. Inhale for 3 counts, exhale for 6 counts. Feel your body relax. See a shaft of white light beaming from the heavens, surrounding your body. Feel in your heart the blessings in your life. Call in your angels, asking for and expressing gratitude.

Visualize a point about 2" below your belly button. See an orange ball of light glowing.

Allow the energy to grow as you think, "I am safe and cared for," "I care for myself," "I am lovable," and "I express my true self beautifully."

While breathing in, pull energy from the root chakra to the second chakra and let it remain there.

Breathe in and out, staying focused on the growing ball of orange energy with love and patience. "I am blessed." "I am grateful."

Sit in silence and gratitude. When the timer goes off, place your hands over your heart. Place your hands over your eyes.

Insights:

In this meditation, we begin to connect the centers. Each breath is a slow inhale, giving notice to the root chakra as you continue the inhale and land on the second chakra, the sacral chakra. Like the root chakra, this center is connected to being present, centered, and joyful. Depression, addictions, sexual health challenges, and fear of death may indicate an out-of-balance second energy center. Feeling safe, loved, and cared for are benefits of sending love into this center. In Chinese medicine, this area is also known as the lower dan tian (don tee ehn). The dan tian translates as elixir field and grows our vitality. A martial arts master may place her hands over this area to protect her energy from negative people or negative energy. Try putting your hands over this area and sending yourself love when you feel low or unsafe.

"It's no use going back to yesterday because I was a different person then."

- Alice in Wonderland

Day 12

Set your timer for 8 minutes

Positive Thoughts:

"I know who I am"

"I am proud of myself"

Begin your meditation in your new space after setting a peaceful scene. Close your eyes. Do 3 Buddha belly breaths. Inhale for 3 counts, exhale for 6 counts. Feel your body relax. See a shaft of white light beaming from the heavens, surrounding your body. Feel in your heart the blessings in your life. Call in your angels, asking for and expressing gratitude for their blessing.

Visualize a point in your stomach area, upper abdomen. See a yellow ball of light glowing.

Allow the energy to grow as you think, "I know who I am," "I am proud of myself," and "I love myself fully." Breathe in and out, pulling the energy from the root chakra to the second center, to the sacral chakra above your belly button.

Stay focused on the sacral chakra and your growing ball of yellow energy with love and patience. "I am blessed." "I am grateful."

Sit in silence and gratitude. When the timer goes off, place your hands over your heart. Place your hands over your eyes.

Insights:

Continue the slow inhale, landing on each center momentarily before stopping at the center we are focusing on today.

Think about where the solar plexus chakra center is, just over the stomach. The phrase "what does your gut say" refers to this center and your ability to make decisions. Trust yourself. Trauma may make us doubt our judgment and threaten our ability to make decisions. Or, trauma may make one power-hungry.

Children of addicts, abusers, and narcissists tend to always look outside of themselves before looking to their intuition. They need to take the temperature of the room to know if it is safe or if is someone about to unleash negative behavior. These children/adults need to learn to listen to their gut first and foremost. Spending time in chakra balancing and especially in the sacral chakra is tremendously helpful. To recover from trauma, you not only need to know who you are but trust yourself and your decisions. Healing this center helps you reclaim your personal power in your life.

"When I despair, I remember that all through history the way of truth and love has always won. There have been tyrants and murderers and for a time they seem invincible, but in the end, they always fall… think of it, always." - Mahatma Gandhi

Day 13

Set your timer for 9 minutes

Positive Thoughts:

"I give and receive love easily"

Begin your meditation in your new space after setting a peaceful scene. Close your eyes. Do 3 Buddha belly breaths. Inhale for 3 counts, exhale for 6 counts. Feel your body relax. See a shaft of white light beaming from the heavens, surrounding your body. Feel in your heart the blessings in your life. Call in your angels, asking for and expressing gratitude for their blessing.

Visualize a point in the center of your chest, at the sternum. See a green ball of light glowing. Allow the energy to grow as you think, "I give and receive love easily," "I love myself," "I can trust others," and "I receive gifts gracefully."

Breathe in and out, pulling the energy from the root chakra to the sacral center, to the solar plexus, and into the heart chakra.

Breathe in and out, staying focused on the heart chakra and your growing ball of green energy with love and patience. "I am blessed." "I am grateful."

Sit in silence and gratitude. When the timer goes off, place your hands over your heart. Place your hands over your eyes.

Insights:

Did you know the heart's electric field is 60 times greater and has an electromagnetic energy field 5000 times greater than the brain's span? Ever been around someone who just makes you feel loved by their very presence? Their heart's energy can be detected to reach three feet outside the physical body. Opening our hearts influences physical health, emotional happiness, and spiritual receptivity. Mystics and meditators spend days, weeks, and years learning to open their heart. Tune into your heart and trust its wisdom. When the heart and brain work in tandem, we become powerful beings.

All the energy centers/chakras have fronts and backs. They move, breathe, give, and receive. To give love, we need to receive love gracefully. To care for others, we need to allow others to care for us. To be cared for, we must also be sensitive to the needs of others. Do you see the give and take, the front and back of each emotion? I am great at taking care of others but was not good at receiving gifts, attention, and compliments. I have learned to say thank you with an open heart.

"No Mud, No Lotus." - Thich Nhat Hanh

Day 14

Set your timer for 10 minutes

Positive Thoughts:

"I am safe to express my truth"

Begin your meditation in your new space after setting a peaceful scene. Close your eyes. Do 3 Buddha belly breaths. Inhale for 3 counts, exhale for 6 counts. Feel your body relax. See a shaft of white light beaming from the heavens, surrounding your body. Feel in your heart the blessings in your life. Call in your angels, asking for and expressing gratitude for their blessing.

Visualize a point at the center of the throat. See a light blue ball of light glowing.

Allow the energy to grow as you think "I am safe to express my truth", or "I find the words to clearly communicate".

Breathe in and out, pulling the energy from the first chakra to the second chakra, to the third chakra, to the fourth chakra, and resting on the throat chakra.

Breathe in and out staying focused on the throat chakra and your growing ball of light blue energy with love and patience. "I speak my truth". "I am seen and heard".

Sit in silence and gratitude. When the timer goes off, place your hands over your heart. Place your hands over your eyes.

Insights:

Speaking one's truth can be done simply when appropriate or necessary. Opening and balancing a throat chakra means you have enough clarity to know and speak your truth. You must also feel safe and confident to be yourself. You must also have enough empathy to speak your truth with love and kindness. After trauma, you may feel unseen and unheard. You may need to scream to the world WTF?! You may completely retreat into a hole to purposefully be unseen and unheard and therefore safe. Be patient and loving with yourself as opening a throat chakra occurs organically and at its own pace.

Some folks need to repeat their trauma story often and to anyone. Be aware of the habit of telling people more than they need to know. Some people never want to tell their stories. They keep their story and emotions held tightly inside. Balance is our goal here. Both are symptoms of an imbalanced throat chakra.

Feeling safe to speak your truth helps heal trauma. Getting thoughts out of the spinning wheel of your head and onto paper, into the universe, or to a friend's ear is part of the process of releasing, understanding, and healing trauma. Speaking one's truth can be with your voice, with art, or in journaling. Journaling opens the energy to a balanced throat chakra and maybe a beautiful place to start. Sit and write and write. Don't edit or overthink it. Burn it when you are done if that feels safer for you. Or, save it to gain perspective down the road.

Singing also opens the energy here, using someone else's words to express your feelings. You don't have to be a great singer or a great artist to open your throat chakra and create.

At this point, we can begin to see how each chakra/energy center connects to the other. We must feel safe, loved, and grounded to fully open our heart and express our heart's truth. As we balance the first center, we feed and balance the second, and so on. This building connection is one reason we need patience with ourselves and our path. For example, maybe the first chakra doesn't balance so easily, but the second is nice and strong, the third is weak and the fourth is closed. Then the throat chakra may be as opened as it can be given the health of the rest of the centers. As the first center becomes balanced, the second is strong, the third becomes stronger, the heart opens, and a new truth comes forth in your life.

"So often it happens that we live our lives in chains and we never even know we have the key." - Already Gone, the Eagles

Day 15

Set your timer for 10 minutes

Positive Thoughts:

"I trust my inner voice"

Begin your meditation in your new space after setting a peaceful scene. Close your eyes. Do 3 Buddha belly breaths. Inhale for 3 counts, exhale for 6 counts. Feel your body relax. See a shaft of white light beaming from the heavens, surrounding your body. Feel in your heart the blessings in your life. Call in your angels, asking for and expressing gratitude for their blessing.

Breathe in quickly and sharply through your nose, and exhale. Visualize a point between your ears, at the back of the throat.

Breathe in sharply through your nose, and exhale. See an infinity symbol in the center of your brain.

Allow the energy to flow as you think "I trust my inner voice", "I connect with wisdom from the universe", or "I see the big picture of my life".

Breathe in sharply through your nose, and exhale. Stay focused on the pineal gland in your brain and the flowing infinity symbol with love and patience. "I am blessed". "I am grateful".

Sit in silence and gratitude. When the timer goes off, place your hands over your heart. Place your hands over your eyes.

Insights:

Note that we change from growing an energy ball and switch to allowing the energy to open and flow. Now our energy focus is not on creating energy but on connecting to energy flow outside of ourselves. At this energy spot, the issue is a fairly universal blockage to be released through breathwork and visualization.

I deviate from the normal chakra flow at this point. Many others will note the next chakra as the third eye. I connect the third eye to the pineal gland, between the ears, and in the center of your head. The pineal gland is a little pinecone-shaped gland, responsible for melatonin production which helps us sleep well. Trauma survivors experience sleep disturbances such as too much sleep or insomnia.

In the mystical arts, the pineal gland relates to our concept of the third eye and spiritual awakening and awareness. Think of the pineal gland as a little radio receiver connected to all the wisdom of the universe. Most of us don't have our little radio receiver turned on, but through meditation, breathing techniques, and sound, we can activate it. Becoming aware of the entire universe gives us perspective on the trauma of our life at this moment in time. We can become aware of a much bigger picture.

There is a Chinese saying describing a person as a frog at the bottom of a well. The frog looks up and sees the sky and thinks it understands the sky. But really the frog just understands a small portion of the sky. Maybe there is a bigger picture to your trauma and life. By feeling the connection to Universal Love and bigger energy in the universe you see that there is a bigger perspective. So, keep tuning your radio receiver to find messages of love and support.

"Breathing in, I calm my body. Breathing out, I smile. Dwelling in the present moment, I know this is a wonderful moment." – Thich Nhat Hahn

Day 16

Set your timer for 15 minutes

Positive Thoughts:

"I live in light and love"

Begin your meditation in your new space after setting a peaceful scene. Close your eyes. Do 3 Buddha belly breaths. Inhale for 3 counts, exhale for 6 counts. Feel your body relax. See a shaft of white light beaming from the heavens, surrounding your body. Feel in your heart the blessings in your life. Call in your angels, asking for and expressing gratitude for their blessing.

With breath in, pull your energy from your feet into your root chakra. Allow it to grow as you affirm, "All my needs and wants are taken care of ".

With breath in, pull your energy from your feet into your root chakra and to the area just below the belly button. Allow it to grow as you affirm, "I am safe and cared for".

With breath in, pull your energy from your feet into your root chakra, to the area just below the belly button, and then to the sacral chakra. Allow it to grow as you affirm, "I know who I am, and I am proud of myself".

With breath in, pull your energy from your feet into your root chakra, to the area just below the belly button, to the sacral chakra, and then to the heart.

Hold the energy there and allow your heart to open as you affirm "I am love".

With breath in, pull your energy from your feet into your root chakra, to the area just below the belly button, to the sacral chakra, to the heart, and then to the throat. Allow the energy to grow as you affirm, "I am safe to express my truth".

With breath in, pull your energy from your feet into your root chakra, to the area just below the belly button, to the sacral chakra, to the heart, to the throat, and then into the pineal gland, between your ears. Allow the energy to open as you affirm, "I trust my inner voice".

With breath in, pull your energy from your feet into your root chakra, to the area just below the belly button, to the stomach area, to the heart, to the throat, into the pineal gland, and to the top of your head. Allow the energy to open as you affirm, "I live in light and love".

Repeat breathing pulling energy from feet to head through your chakras.

Sit in silence and gratitude. When the timer goes off, place your hands over your heart. Place your hands over your eyes.

Insights:

The breaths in this meditation do not need to be immediate. You can take many breaths, but each visualization begins with an inhale, pulling your energy up through the centers, and landing on a specific area of focus. Breathe with energy. Breathe with the energy needed to create your new world. Breathe with joy. Breathe with the joy you are bringing into your life.

We end with the crown chakra, at the top of your head. The crown chakra acknowledges our connection to God, the angels, and the bigger universe. Allow the blessings and protection of your angels and spirit guides to envelope you in white light from your crown chakra to your entire body. Love is the most powerful force in the universe. Embrace the love within you and around you. Now, let the energy flow from the crown chakra back to mother Earth and up again.

Torus

From my perspective, when I am doing the chakra/energy center meditations I am also vitalizing an energy torus healing. A torus is like a donut of energy always moving around you. As you are breathing up through the chakras and the center of your body the energy moves with you and continues up to the 8th center above your head and then back down into the earth. With practice, you can feel and control the energy through your breathing and intention. You can also make the energy move from the top of your head, down through the center of your body, and back into Earth.

I see the energy entering Earth, to receive her vitality, up between my legs, up the center of my torso through the chakras, up to the 8th center, and then cascading down, creating a protective field, re-entering Earth to be brought back up again. Your breath and intention should be focused and strong. This exercise energizes and sharpens the mind and body.

"Everyone is a genius; but if you judge a fish by its ability to climb a tree, it will spend its whole life thinking it is stupid." - Albert Einstein

Day 17

Set your timer for 15 minutes

Positive Thoughts:

"I see today as better than yesterday"

Today's meditation is a journaling meditation.

Today, in your peaceful place, let your words flow from your mind onto paper.

Acknowledge past mindsets that you are releasing.

Acknowledge changes you are proud of.

See progress in your life.

Recognize the areas you will change in behavior or thought patterns.

Recognize personality strengths that are serving you well.

Let the words flow, unjudged, unedited. You don't need to read these words or even keep them. When done writing, you can keep the paper or destroy the paper and move on. No need to dwell, just acknowledge and release.

Insights:

For some reason, we humans forget about resolved issues quickly and keep focusing on the failures or challenges, forgetting the amazingly positive things in the past. We look at the mountains ahead and forget to be proud of the climb behind us. Today I want you to recognize accomplishments, identify mountains, complement yourself for your strengths.

This journaling meditation helps keep us focused on accomplishments while also focusing on accomplishments to come.

The magician's word "Abracadabra" comes
from an Aramaic phrase "avra kehdabra"

and means "I will create as I speak".

Day 18

Set your timer for 15 minutes

Positive Thoughts:

"I AM"

Begin your meditation in your new space after setting a peaceful scene. Close your eyes. Do 3 Buddha belly breaths. Inhale for 3 counts, exhale for 6 counts. Visualize your happy place. Feel your body relax. See a shaft of white light beaming from the heavens, surrounding your body. Feel in your heart the blessings in your life. Call in your angels, asking for and expressing gratitude for their blessing.

In your mind repeat, "I Am". When you are inspired, add "I am …... "(for example, I am happy). Then go back to thinking "I Am". Again, when you are inspired, add "I am…". Keep doing this throughout the meditation with your breath slowly and joyfully.

Sit in silence and gratitude. When the timer goes off, place your hands over your heart. Place your hands over your eyes.

Insights:

Today, we are learning the power of "I am" statements. Negative self-talk pops up often in beginning meditation, especially after trauma. Finding positive thoughts, hope and self-esteem are vital to creating a peaceful, happy life.

"I am" statements are more than positive affirmations, however. In the book of Exodus, when Moses was asked God's name, he replied *Ehyeh asher ehyeh* which translates for some as "I am that I am". We all have God/Source/Universal Love within us. We are all part of this universe and connected to each other throughout space and time. Dr. Wayne Dyer says never speak of yourself with any words you wouldn't also use to describe God. You have God within you and to describe yourself as something negative is also describing God as something negative.

For some people, the light of God is within them but is really, really small. For others, the light of God shines bright with love. While reciting your "I am" mantra, open your heart and connect with the source of love. Know you are part of something much bigger and better than the circumstances you find yourself in right now.

"Do not speak bad of yourself. For the warrior within hears your words and is lessened by them." - Japanese samurai proverb

Day 19

Set your timer for 20 minutes or more

Positive Thoughts:

"My story is a happy story"

Today's meditation is a journaling meditation.

Write the story of your life so far. Read the story and rewrite any elements that don't ring true for you. Now write the ending of your story. Write your ending as you want it to happen. Remember, this ending is about you, not others. What happens to you? Keep away from endings like "my ex dies in a fiery car crash". Your story isn't about your ex, it is about you living a happy life full of love and joy.

Writing your story after trauma is a journey of healing. In the beginning, the trauma and pain may take center stage. If your trauma is fresh and raw, honor the pain. Eventually, the story of your strong beautiful spirit becomes the overriding theme. One magical day your trauma becomes a side note to a story of triumph.

Dare to imagine and be bold. Let the Universe figure out how it will happen, you don't need to get bogged down in logistics. Find your story of success and pride and write it.

"All things are possible. Who you are is limited by who you think you are."

- Egyptian Book of the Dead

The Power of "I don't know"

When we begin healing and recreating our life, we must believe in a possibility. Everything is possible. It is not our job to figure out how to heal, how our life is going to take shape again. The Universe will figure out the how. Our job is to imagine the life we want and then allow the Universe to create it. We need to be open to receiving. Other meditation practitioners will tell you; that they received their wishes when they detached from the results. They put their desires out there and let them go. An attitude similar to the traditional wisdom that you will fall in love when you stop looking for it.

It is much easier to detach from results when life is basically fine. When you are lacking housing, food, health, and other basics of survival, detaching is much more difficult. For me, I found the detachment in "I don't know". A point came for me when my meditations were great, my spirit was happy, and I smiled at life. I didn't have an income stream. What am I going to do for money? "I don't know". With each "I don't know" my spirit soared with faith and trust in the Universe. Don't get me wrong. I was job hunting, putting the effort into creating. But I know the real magic will come out of a split-second inspiration guided by my angels. I have created my future and I trust in the timing and path. I will see the path if I am aligned and in tune with myself and my environment. For now, focus on gratitude and the beauty you can see, forget about the stresses, and joyfully trust.

Day 20

Set your timer for 17 minutes

Positive Thoughts:

"I am a beautiful person with a beautiful heart"

Begin your meditation in your new space after setting a peaceful scene. Close your eyes. Do 3 Buddha belly breaths. Inhale for 3 counts, exhale for 6 counts. Visualize your happy place. Feel your body relax. See a shaft of white light beaming from the heavens, surrounding your body. Feel in your heart the blessings in your life. Call in your angels, asking for and expressing gratitude for their blessing.

Place your hands over your belly, just below the belly button.

With breath in, slowly move your hands to just above your left breast area and at the same time, turn your head to the left.

With breath out, move your hands to your heart chakra and move your head to face forward.

With breath in, turn your head to the right and move your hands to just above your right breast area.

With breath out return your hands to your belly button area and move your head to face forward.

Repeat this movement as many times as you like. Breaks of stillness with hands at the belly button area are encouraged. Move slowly.

Sit in silence and gratitude. When the timer goes off, place your hands over your heart. Place your hands over your eyes.

Insights:

This meditation is a Qigong meditation. In this meditation, the movement of your hands is drawing a big heart on your chest. This meditation is designed to connect your Kidney Qi with your Heart Qi and Lung Qi. As I wrote earlier in the book, when I speak of Kidney Qi, I am not really talking about your physical kidneys as western medicine knows it. We are speaking of the Chinese meridian systems and the energy that flows through them. Connecting Kidney Qi, Heart Qi, and Lung Qi with love is calming and energizing. The emotion of Kidney Qi is fear, Heart Qi is anxiety and is part of all emotions, and Lung Qi is grief. All these emotions and trauma go hand in hand. This meditation balances and strengthens these organ systems and their corresponding emotion. As you strengthen your Kidney Qi, you are not as fearful. As you strengthen and honor your heart, you calm anxiety. As you breathe out, you release grief. This meditation balances and connects Heart Qi with Lung Qi and Kidney Qi. You might feel more grounded, more focused, or able to breathe easier after this meditation.

Our life's purpose is not a tangible goal.

Our life's purpose is the beauty of our heart's expression.

Day 21

Set your timer for 18 minutes

Positive Thoughts:

"My heart is open"

Begin your meditation in your new space after setting a peaceful scene. Close your eyes. Do 3 Buddha belly breaths. Inhale for 3 counts, exhale for 6 counts. Visualize your happy place. Feel your body relax. See a shaft of white light beaming from the heavens, surrounding your body. Feel in your heart the blessings in your life. Call in your angels, asking for and expressing gratitude for their blessing.

Turn your attention to your heart center. How does it feel? Honor whatever description or thought may arise. Do you feel any vibrations there? Can you feel any pulsing? What color is it? Do you have any emotions attached to it? Keep your attention on your heart center.

Visualize your heart center with an image such as a lotus, sunlight, or your puppy's face. Something that makes you happy and full of love. Stay with that love. Allow the love and gratitude to grow all around you. Begin breathing in and out of your heart center. Let love grow and fill you. Think about how much you love something.

Sit in silence and gratitude. When the timer goes off, place your hands over your heart. Place your hands over your eyes.

Insights:

We are continuing to connect with our heart, connect our heart with our mind. Being absolutely comfortable in the stillness of the Universe is one of the greatest feelings of peace and joy you will ever experience. I realize that when I recommend breathing in and out of the heart, many folks will go "Huh?". Feeling energy, vibrations, and breathing in and out of the heart are all difficult to explain. Then one day, you feel it, you get it. For now, see your breath flowing in and out of your heart similar to your breath flowing in and out of your nose or mouth. If you haven't felt your heart's breath yet, just keep trying till one day, you make it. Keep visualizing, keep trying. Try not to judge or minimalize any thoughts or feelings you experience.

"It's impossible," said pride.
"It's risky," said experience.
"It's pointless," said reason.
"Give it a try," whispered the heart.
-   Unknown

Self-Care Simplified

Taking care of yourself is why you are reading this book. I want to talk a bit about different ways you can care for yourself. The best self-care in my opinion is about being mindful in your life.

I have been that natural health person on a strict diet of superfoods, vegan, gluten-free, a strict life of control and denial. After 30 years of practice, I have concluded that happiness is way more important than being overly concerned with diet. Ability to handle stress, laugh easily, and know your priorities in life are the best medicines there are. I am not suggesting you alter your life if you have real allergies or medical conditions, but do prioritize how you eat, how you breathe, and how you laugh as much as what you eat.

Ways to increase happy brain chemicals:

- Dopamine, the feel-good neurotransmitter. Dopamine is stimulated by eating foods we crave or with sex. Dopamine is so awesome it can trigger certain addictive behaviors. Stimulate dopamine naturally by eating seeds, nuts, lentils, cheese, and meats, getting good sleep and daily exercise, and through meditation, visualization, and breathing exercises.

- Oxytocin is the love hormone, increased in the beginning stages of falling in love. Oxytocin reduces stress and anxiety. Oxytocin is easily stimulated by hugs, giving compliments, pets, yoga, music, and meditation.
- Serotonin is the happiness and mood stabilizer neurotransmitter. Serotonin is increased naturally with certain food combinations like oatmeal and nuts or salmon and brown rice. Exercise, sunshine, and meditation are other ways to increase serotonin naturally.
- Endorphins can decrease pain and increase happiness. Endorphins increase with laughter, dark chocolate, wine, exercise, acupuncture, and meditation.

Did you notice that meditation made all the lists of ways to increase happy brain chemicals?!! Exercise, eat well, get some sunshine, and meditate to help your brain help you to be happy.

"Never go to sleep feeling discouraged or dissatisfied.

Never sleep in the consciousness of failure."

- Neville Goddard

Water Essentials

Water contains vibration and as meditators, we are attuning our bodies to a higher vibration. Dr. Masaru Emoto photographed the crystals formed in frozen water when specific thoughts are directed toward them. The photos exemplify the beauty of the water that has been exposed to loving words. In contrast, water exposed to negative thoughts were incoherent, asymmetrical patterns with dull colors. Our bodies are 75% water. The Earth is 50% water. The implication is shifting the water we consume and the water in our body to a state of positive, loving vibration will positively create a new you and new Earth. Today, bless the water you are drinking, bless yourself and feel the beauty.

Trauma can affect digestion and the ability to drink water. Often, trauma makes a person nauseous or bloated after drinking water. Keep drinking good liquids by also drinking green or black tea, room temperature water, or by adding a few drops of lemon to the water to make it tastier and easier to drink. Avoid artificial sweeteners and ingredients. Bless each bottle or glass of water with intentions of love and healing, then drink in the magic.

Day 22

Set your timer for 20 minutes

Positive Thoughts:

"I am aligned with my higher self"

Begin your meditation in your new space after setting a peaceful scene. Close your eyes. Do 3 Buddha belly breaths. Inhale for 3 counts, exhale for 6 counts. Visualize your happy place. Feel your body relax. See a shaft of white light beaming from the heavens, surrounding your body. Feel in your heart the blessings in your life. Call in your angels, asking for and expressing gratitude for their blessing.

In your mind, see your body floating up above Earth. You are safe.

Float through the atmosphere into the blackness of space. You can see the Earth below growing smaller. The blackness of space surrounds you. Peaceful silence is all you hear. Allow yourself to be comfortable just being in space, surrounded in all directions by blackness.

Slowly focus on your heart. Breathe into your heart. Breathe out from the heart.

Connect your heart to God/Source love by asking, "What is the vibration of Source Love?"

Allow Source love into your body and life.

Connect to your Higher self by saying, "I acknowledge my Higher Self and align with my Higher Self". Feel yourself connected with an energy bigger than you. An energy that knows you and connects with you easily. An energy full of love and possibility. Dissolve your body into this Higher Self energy.

Now you are no longer your body in space but a larger energy of love and light. This larger energy of love and light has an even bigger connection to Source Love. Welcome the energy and blessings into your body. Slowly return to Earth.

Sit in stillness and gratitude and end with "I am blessed", or "I am grateful". Place your hands over your heart. Place your hands over your face.

Insights:

Today our imagination must get bigger than our Earthly senses and experiences prepare us for. Today, you must see yourself disappearing into the darkness and connecting with your Higher Self. What is a Higher Self? Your Higher Self is another aspect of you, vested in your happiness, like your guardian angels. Your Higher Self and you are one. Connect with this energy to begin developing the skill of creation. We are all meant to be joyful, happy, loving beings on the beautiful planet Earth. At some point, we drifted away from this mission. Through meditation and creation, we return to the mission of joy.

For one minute, walk outside, and stand there in silence.

Look up at the sky and contemplate how amazing life is.

Day 23

Set your timer for 20 minutes

Positive Thoughts:

"I choose health, wealth, and happiness"

Begin your meditation in your new space after setting a peaceful scene. Close your eyes. Do 3 Buddha belly breaths. Inhale for 3 counts, exhale for 6 counts. Feel your body relax.

In your mind's eye, see a wall made of felt. On the floor is a pile of numbers.

Pick up the number 10 and place it on the wall. Take your time and see each step. Say "10".

Pick up the number 9 and place it on the wall. Say "9".

Continue this process until you have placed all 10 numbers on the wall. Feel a sense of accomplishment and pride.

Then in reverse order, remove the numbers. Remove number 1. Remove number 2 and so on until the wall is blank. Feel more accomplishment with the relaxation of knowing you are a capable, strong person.

Now, notice a pile of pictures on the floor. There are pictures of apples, kittens, houses, cars, people skiing, people doing yoga, and so on. Choose the picture that represents health to you. Place that picture on the wall.

Choose a picture that represents wealth and place it on the wall.

Choose a picture that represents happiness and place it on the wall.

Look at the pictures on the wall and think "I choose health, wealth, and happiness". Say this three times.

Remove each picture one by one. As you remove it think, "I choose …. " and then place the picture in your pocket.

Remove each picture one by one. Place them in your pocket and keep them with you.

Sit in stillness and gratitude and end with "I am blessed", or "I am grateful". Place your hands over your heart. Place your hands over your face.

Insights:

This type of meditation is a form of self-hypnosis. Seeing the actions slowly, and associating pictures and words help us get past some self-limiting beliefs to reprogram the subconscious into positive thought patterns. Just doing the beginning part of the meditation with the numbers can slow the heart rate and ease anxiety. By also incorporating positive choices of our own definition, we begin replacing trauma with new choices, and new visualizations. For example, a motorhome is my symbol of financial freedom. When I see a Class C motorhome with no slides and solar panels, I see myself free with all needs and wants met. I choose this financial freedom. I keep that picture in my pocket and know it is mine. I am replacing poverty with financial freedom. I am not going to look at poverty again, it is in my past. Financial freedom is my choice. Keep building.

"Try squeezing a handful of water and see how quickly it disappears. But relax, and let your hand flow in the same water, and you have the experience of the water as long as you like." – Dr. Wayne Dyer

Day 24

Set your timer for 20 minutes

Positive Thoughts:

"I am blessed with love"

Begin your meditation in your new space after setting a peaceful scene. Close your eyes. Do 3 Buddha belly breaths. Inhale for 3 counts, exhale for 6 counts. Visualize your happy place. Feel your body relax. See a shaft of white light beaming from the heavens, surrounding your body. Feel in your heart the blessings in your life. Call in your angels, asking for and expressing gratitude for their blessing.

In your mind, see your body floating up above Earth. You are safe.

Float through the atmosphere into the blackness of space. You can see the Earth below growing smaller. The blackness of space surrounds you. Peaceful silence is all you hear.

Allow yourself to be comfortable just being in space, surrounded in all directions by blackness.

Slowly focus on your heart. Breathe into your heart. Breathe out from the heart.

Slowly focus on your pineal gland. Feel the vibrations around you in the blackness.

Slowly focus on your 7th chakra. Connect to God/Source love by asking, "What is the vibration of

Source Love?" Allow any feelings or intuitions to arise. Acknowledge them and stay focused on the vibrations of Source Love. Welcome the energy and blessings into your body.

Remain in the blackness.

Picture yourself as magnetically attracting all the beauty, love, health, wealth, and joy you desire. Each gift finds its way into your life. This takes no effort for you. Just relax and be the magnet for gifts. The gifts will take the path of least resistance to come into your life. You relax and allow the gifts to become a part of you. Breathe into the relaxation of knowing. Knowing all you desire is yours. Trust. Faith. Patience. Gratitude.

Slowly return to Earth.

Sit in silence and gratitude. When the timer goes off, place your hands over your heart. Place your hands over your eyes.

Insights:

Today we continue introducing you to the concept of the blackness. The void, the quantum field, the 5th dimension, and the blackness are all concepts of another dimension in space we can access with our mind. In this blackness, we can access another level of information and creation. Everyone can do this. In this blackness, all events and vibrations exist. There is no end. Space is unlimited, never-ending. Everything is possible.

Today you accessed the blackness and connected with the love of God, Source Love. You are loved. You are important. Receive the love into your body and life. Allow and trust everything gets better every day. In Love, we create health and happiness.

"Never by hatred is hatred conquered, but by readiness to love alone. This is eternal law."
- Buddha

Day 25

Set your timer for 20 minutes

Positive Thoughts

"I am worthy"

Begin your meditation in your new space after setting a peaceful scene. Close your eyes. Do 3 Buddha belly breaths. Inhale for 3 counts, exhale for 6 counts. Visualize your happy place. Feel your body relax. See a shaft of white light beaming from the heavens, surrounding your body. Feel in your heart the blessings in your life. Call in your angels, asking for and expressing gratitude for their blessing.

Go to the blackness.

See yourself as you want to be. Visualize yourself in a happy, healthy moment. Feel the warmth of joy spread through your body.

Stay in the blackness.

See the world around you in all its beauty. Feel the love you receive and give.

Be grateful.

Stay in this moment as long as you can. Attach any shame, unworthiness, or negative thoughts to balloons and release them from your life. Be the person of love and light, living a joyful moment.

Sit in stillness and gratitude and end with "I am blessed", or "I am grateful".

Insights:

This meditation is about letting go of feelings of unworthiness and embracing joy. In trauma, we may feel we are worthy of bad things happening in our life and unworthy of good things. This thought isn't true. I absolutely know you are worthy of joy. You are worthy of all that you need. You are worthy of all good things. All good things happen to you today.

There was an upworthy post on Instagram one day from StressieBessie about her young son's advice on life. I thought it was fabulous advice. 1. You gotta say your affirmations in your mouth and your heart. You say "I am brave of this meeting!", "I am loved!", "I smell good!" And you can say five or three or ten until you know it. 2. You gotta walk big. You gotta mean it. Like Dolly on a dinosaur. Because you got it. 3. Never put a skunk on a bus. 4. Think about the donuts of your day! Even if you cry a little, you can think about potato chips!

The wisdom of a child is within each of us. Sometimes life knocks us about and we forget the pure joy of this life. Negative words and experiences loom larger than positive words. This meditation is about seeing those negative thoughts in your subconscious, in your body (remember our muscles hold memories) and in your self-talk. Attach them to balloons and release. Go big,

go love, go donuts! You are worthy of every good
thing you can imagine.

"Your task is not to seek for love, but merely to seek and find all the barriers within yourself that you have built against it." — *Rumi*

"The wound is the place where the Light enters you." — *Rumi*

Day 26

Set your timer for 20 minutes

Positive Thoughts:

"I am one with Earth"

Begin your meditation in your new space after setting
a peaceful scene. Close your eyes. Do 3 Buddha
belly breaths. Inhale for 3 counts, exhale for 6 counts.
Visualize your happy place. Feel your body relax. See
a shaft of white light beaming from the heavens,
surrounding your body. Feel in your heart the
blessings in your life. Call in your angels, asking for
and expressing gratitude for their blessing.

Visualize the planet Earth. Allow your mind to wander
to parts of Earth: plants, animals, water, etc.

As you see each aspect, see it as happy and joyful.
The tree is strong and nourished. The dolphins' dance
and play. The flower blooms in the sun. A field of
wheat sways in the breeze beneath a beautiful
rainbow. A dandelion grows in the crack of the
sidewalk.

Bless each aspect with love and light.

See Earth. See her as a being of Universal Love.
Breathe in rhythm with Earth. Bless Earth and all
beings of Light and Love dwelling upon her.

Sit in stillness and gratitude and end with "I am
blessed", or "I am grateful".

Insights:

Chinese medicine is based on the idea that what happens in nature, happens in our body. We are microcosms of the Universe and interconnected with nature. Microcosm means we are the small world, a reflection of the larger world. As each of us is part of God, part of Universal Source Love, so is Earth. We are part of Earth; Earth is part of us. By healing Earth, we heal ourselves. We can only be as healthy and happy as Earth. We are taking the love and energy we are developing for yourself and extending it to the planet we live on, laugh on, and need for survival. By healing our planet, we heal ourselves.

"The more you understand, the more you love. The more you love, the more you understand." – Thich Nhat Hanh

Dimensions Simplified

We live in a three-dimension world. We can measure, touch, feel, taste, and smell our environment and we experience time in a linear format. Meditation as I am describing it explores concepts of additional dimensions, or what used to be called planes of existence.

What I want you to begin to understand is meditation is going far beyond relaxing you. By entering the blackness, we are accessing another dimension. By visualizing and feeling in this place of blackness, we begin creation. By feeling gratitude, we pull that creation into our life. Neville Goddard recommends going to sleep every night assuming all your wishes coming true. And eventually, they will be.

The theory goes, that as you increase your energy, and raise your vibration, then you can access higher dimensions of reality. Higher dimensions of reality can be analogous to being closer to God in that infinite Love is available. We connect with a new plane of existence that is always there and is accessible to all, we just haven't connected with it yet. In this new dimension, our 3D life is altered. We create our reality in the 5D through meditation. We allow that creation into the 3D by meditation, gratitude, and joy. Some have put forth the idea that if many of us raise our vibration on earth, then earth too can enter another dimension and earth's healing can also be created.

When you haven't gone there it is hard to imagine there is a 5th dimension to reality. I'm a skeptic. But

I'm also open-minded and curious. Imagine the sailors who tried to convince other sailors that they weren't going to fall off the earth's edge by sailing just a bit farther. Be that brave sailor, curious about possibilities.

Let's say your trauma is an illness. You can go into the 5th dimension and see a healthy you and then experience a healthy you in your world, verified by your medical doctor. There are hundreds of testimonials describing this success of healing through meditation and working with other dimensions of reality. Hundreds of testimonials crediting the gift of infinite Love's healing as well.

What if your trauma is grief and the loss of a spouse? You can't go into the 5th dimension and get your spouse back. But you can learn a new perspective on death, develop a new relationship with your spouse, and see and create a happy life again.

For centuries teachers have taught meditation techniques for creating health, and happiness, yet we didn't learn it so well. However, I believe now is the time for Earth and humankind to reclaim joy and love. And I see meditation as an amazing tool to do this.

Here's the thing though, I have done these meditations pre-trauma and post-trauma and then again after another trauma. It's harder and slower for me this last time in some ways. My faith faltered. My fatigue increased. My ego suffered. I started giving up. Recovering from trauma is hard. Our effort isn't spent attracting some shiny new toy, our effort is spent not crying, not dying, recovering hope. I was talking to a friend about this book and mentioned that I will be taken more seriously when I have more outer signs of "success". She scolded me and reframed my situation. I am alive and healthy. I am happy. I am loved and I love. I am grateful. I look forward to the day every morning. I laugh easily. These are my major accomplishments, and I am proud of them.

I am not healthy because of medications or my diet. I am healthy in part because I trained my mind to be in control of my body and life through meditation. I created a healthy body in the 5th dimension and brought it into my life. Through meditation, I expanded my understanding of life on Earth and have a closer connection to Universal Love. Life will send me new traumas and stresses from time to time. That's ok, I can handle it and find a new magical journey in each event.

Eventually, with all my meditation practices and growth, I will die. Death is not a failure. We all die. Death is a transition, a moving on, a new beginning. I have been clinically dead twice in my life and know it to be a peaceful event. Death is not a failure of meditation, visualization, or other practices. My meditation practices have allowed me more time to do more things but do not prevent the final result we all meet at some point.

Day 27

Set your timer for 30 minutes

Positive Thoughts:

"I envision my life"

Today's meditation is a journaling day meditation.

Today we connect with creating our heart's desire. Get a pen, crayon, paint, and/or paper and begin describing your life's creation. Manifestation techniques can be journaling, art, collage, and more. I do a yearly manifestation with my kids each New Year's Day. We get a piece of paper and take turns writing or drawing something we bring into the New Year. We bring in art lessons, dance lessons, health, happiness, new pets, and wealth. We give those wishes a symbol and keep it on the fridge.

Today I want you to begin writing and drawing the elements of your life. Maybe you already have them, maybe you are bringing them into your life. A few suggestions, make all sentences present tense and positive. The Universe does not understand negative phrases. For example, if you write "I don't want any more jerks in my life" the Universe hears "I want more jerks in my life". Instead, try "The people in my life are positive, honest, and love-based." Also, be specific on the things that matter. You don't just want a new house, you want a new house in a safe, happy community. When you aren't sure, be general. One year I listed that I wanted a life full of giggles and butterflies. That was the year my first daughter was born.

You can focus just on one area, like health, wealth, or happiness, or list the whole picture. Don't feel that if you don't list it, you won't get it. You can do this a thousand times and pull in all the aspects of your life. This is a journey, not an event. If you are having dental problems, visualize the jaw and teeth of a shark or pit bull, strong and healthy. If you need more money, visualize a pen, and see yourself writing checks with ease, releasing you from all debt.

While I want you to know that everything is possible, everything does need to be in your best interest. One person was sure this was all silly. He had been visualizing a $2 million yacht and not received it. He hadn't created a life that would sustain a huge yacht. It wasn't in his best interest. He was trying to do magic, twitch his nose, and make something appear. Create the next step on your journey. Trust in the divine knowledge and keep building your dream life.

Also, this is only about you. You cannot create for anyone else. You cannot create for or control your kids, family, best friend, or spouse. If each person in the world created a life of love and joy and took care of their own journey, we would have a beautiful world.

Now create a symbol for your list. It may be a number, letter, picture, or symbol. Choose one and attached all your healings and creations to this symbol. Now, instead of manifesting a long list, you just need to manifest the symbol.

When you have listed your life creations and given it a symbol, keep it for tomorrow's meditation.

Day 28

Set your timer for 20 minutes. Use the symbol from Day 24 for today's meditation.

Positive Thoughts:

"I am the co-creator of my life"

Begin your meditation in your new space after setting a peaceful scene. Close your eyes. Do 3 Buddha belly breaths. Inhale for 3 counts, exhale for 6 counts. Visualize your happy place. Feel your body relax. See a shaft of white light beaming from the heavens, surrounding your body. Feel in your heart the blessings in your life. Call in your angels, asking for and expressing gratitude for their blessing.

In your mind, see your body floating up above Earth. You are safe. Float through the atmosphere into the blackness of space. You can see the Earth below growing smaller. The blackness of space surrounds you. Peaceful silence is all you hear.

Allow yourself to be comfortable just being in space, surrounded in all directions by blackness.

Slowly focus on your heart. Breathe into your heart. Breathe out from the heart. Connect your heart to God/Source love by asking, "What is the vibration of Source Love?"

Allow Source love into your body and life.

Connect to your Higher self by saying, "I acknowledge my Higher Self and align with my Higher Self". Feel yourself connected with an energy bigger than you.

Dissolve your body into this Higher Self energy. Now you are no longer your body in space but a larger energy of love and light.

See the symbol you created, floating in space. Using your heart energy pull that symbol into your body. Welcome your creation into your heart and into your life. Let the symbol be in your body.

Feel the gratitude of knowing your life has changed, today. Today, you received your wishes, and be in gratitude and joy. Be in gratitude in the darkness as long as you can.

Slowly return to Earth, to your body.

Sit in stillness and gratitude and end with "I am blessed", or "I am grateful".

Insights:

I do this meditation in many ways. Sometimes I do a bit of self-hypnosis and then open a door with my symbol on it, stepping into my new life. Sometimes I let the symbol in space be a door, entering my created life there. Lots of meditation teachers do a variation on this meditation. The point is to consciously know you are a worthy being, full of love and light, envisioning a shift in your life, pulling it into your heart and mind, and trusting that all is perfect right now.

This journey takes time. The first steps are to get into your body, be less triggered by trauma, feel in control of your body, find happiness in the moment. These meditations will absolutely help you on that path. The next steps are to feel part of a bigger magical picture based in love and light. In that picture, you

"There is nothing more important than developing your imagination to transform your life from the inside world of your thoughts and feelings to the outside world of your results and manifestations." - Neville Goddard

Day 29

Set your timer for 20 minutes.

Positive Thoughts:

"I see what is acceptable and what is not acceptable in my life"

"I set boundaries for myself with ease and grace"

Begin your meditation in your new space after setting a peaceful scene. Close your eyes. Do 3 Buddha belly breaths. Inhale for 3 counts, exhale for 6 counts. Feel your body relax. Feel in your heart the blessings in your life. Call in your angels, asking for and expressing gratitude for their blessing.

Surround yourself in a dome of white gauze-like material. There is light and brightness. The dome is large, beautiful, and spacious, encompassing you and your life. You feel safe. Imagine that gauze has the magical ability to release anything negative from your life. Negative thoughts and events can float up from your life and exit your protective dome. Simultaneously, this beautiful, strong, and flexible dome of gauze can also catch and hold any negative thoughts trying to enter your life. If another person attempts to send you bad words or energies, the gauze stops them mid-air and dissolves them into white light to never harm another. You are protected in your gauze dome. You are setting boundaries for what is acceptable in your life. You are releasing old thought patterns, beliefs, and people that are no longer in your best interest. You thrive in this dome. You can raise this dome of protection and releasing at any point in time.

Sit in silence and gratitude. When the timer goes off, place your hands over your heart. Place your hands over your eyes.

Insights:

In this meditation, we use gauze as a protective barrier to set boundaries in our life. We release that which is not serving us. We prevent what is not ok from coming into our life. Setting boundaries is especially important for trauma survivors because trauma usually means something has drastically crossed our boundaries. To heal, we must re-instate healthy boundaries.

Think about what setting a boundary entails.

> To set a boundary you must have a sense of worthiness.

> To set a boundary you must have an idea about what is ok and what is not ok in your life.

> To set a boundary you must trust your own inner voice.

> To set a boundary you must prioritize your inner voice over other people's opinion.

> To set a boundary you must have clarity.

To set a boundary you must care about yourself.

To set a boundary you must feel safe to express your own needs and ideas.

To set a boundary you must feel strong enough to meet any conflict your boundary might create.

Through meditation, you have begun opening your throat chakra, getting in touch with your inner voice, becoming present and aware in your life. Do this meditation for several days. When you are ready, identify areas of your life that may be crossing your boundaries and try setting healthy boundaries.

Knowing what healthy compromise is and what is an overstep of your boundaries must be constantly reviewed. Agreeing to things to just keep the peace is a trauma response. Possibly you are making yourself uncomfortable for others to feel comfortable. Possibly you are giving in to avoid the conflict. Possibly you are agreeing to something you don't want because you don't know what you want. You have control now. You run your life. Take up space and use your voice.

As a side note, in Chinese medicine, cinnamon is one of my favorite herbs with the properties to both release, protect and nourish. Cinnamon can open our energy to let negative energy be released. We see this in the usage of cinnamon in cold and flu formulas like Gui Zhi Tang. Cinnamon also has the ability to warm and nourish us sweetly, gently, and effectively. When we are our weakest, cinnamon can help us recover our strength.

"No person is your friend who demands your silence, or denies your right to grow."

- Alice Walker

Self-Worth

Part of boundary-setting skills entails self-worth. Are you worthy of getting what you want? Some signs of lacking self-worth are:

Basing your worth on people's approval of you.

Making excuses for others' behaviors.

Over-explaining yourself, especially to strangers.

Feeling like you must rationalize your life.

Staying quiet to avoid conflict or rejection.

Criticizing yourself or others too much.

These behaviors are not to be judged are criticized either! Recognize areas that need attention in your life and begin changing yourself and your thought patterns. Just bringing light to a pattern that is not serving you begins to shift the load from unworthy to self-love.

I remember a time I learned the lesson of self-worth and boundaries in a subtle way. I worked in an office that had an L-shaped corridor. Near the bend there were seats. I would sit in those seats taking notes often. Two lovely, yet very "male", co-workers would walk down the hall and always aim at me just enough to make me pull in my feet. In the beginning, I would apologize for being in their way. Then I stopped apologizing. There was a huge hallway they could walk and not come anywhere near me. It was easier to go around me than up to me. Yet, their subconscious need to passively dominate always led them to walk in a way to make me recede. I quit pulling in my feet and just looked at them without judgment. The first couple of times they would actually stop and wait for me to pull in my feet. Then they altered their path and never did it again. Never was a word said. Never did I confront them. They probably still do not realize what was happening. Yet I felt more self-worth at realizing the crossed boundary and correcting it.

"It's your road and yours alone. Others may
walk it with you, but no one can walk it for you."

- Rumi

Day 30

Set your timer for 20 minutes.

Positive Thoughts:

"Flowers are strong"

Begin your meditation in your new space after setting a peaceful scene. Close your eyes. Do 3 Buddha belly breaths. Inhale for 3 counts, exhale for 6 counts. Feel your body relax. Feel in your heart the blessings in your life. Call in your angels, asking for and expressing gratitude for their blessing.

Visualize your favorite flower in your heart's center. See the bloom and beauty opening your heart. Feel the stem descend from your flower, down your torso, and down each leg. The stem is pliable yet strong and nourishing. Feel the roots grow from the ball of your foot into the Earth. Let the roots grow deep into the Earth. With each breath in pull up nourishment from the Earth, into your roots, up the stem and allow that nourishment to feed you and your flower. With each breath out descend your energy down the stem and roots back to the Earth. Breathe in this rhythm for a while. Feel your connection to Mother Earth grounding and nourishing you. Imagine the wind is blowing and your flower can sway in the wind without breaking. Your flower is nourished and strong. You are nourished and strong.

When you are ready, bless yourself, your flower, and Mother Earth. Place your hands over your belly, blessing your core strength, blessing the nourishment you just received.

Place your hands over your heart, blessing your open and strong heart.

Place your hands over your eyes, blessing your strong spirit.

Insights:

I remember once reading a Japanese poem that included the line "Flowers are strong". I no longer can find the poem, but that line has never left me. The biggest storm can come over and the flower remains. Maybe the flower lost a petal or two, but its beauty and life remain intact. Embracing the energy of the flower reminds us that we can endure and yet remain strong and beautiful.

After a traumatic event, we all hear from well-meaning friends, "What doesn't kill you makes you stronger". No, I made myself stronger. I am a survivor of a situation I never wanted. I am a warrior. I met the darkness and turned it into light. I pulled up my energy and found the sun. My trauma situation didn't give me strength. My trauma situation made me realize how much strength I had all along.

The Japanese art of kintsugi repairs broken pottery with a powder of gold lacquer to highlight imperfections. This beautiful art teaches us that broken objects are not something to hide but to display with pride. Turn the cracks into beautiful texture, shine, and depth making what was once broken unique and beautiful.

Connect with the energy of the flower and embrace your own strength and beauty.

"Much of spiritual life is self-acceptance. Maybe all of it." - Jack Kornfield

Success!

I am so pleased you took this journey with me. I hope you got something from these meditations and my life experience. I want to leave you with a few thoughts.

One of the benefits of meditation as a tool in your life is mediating stress. Stress happens in life. Experiencing stress is not a failure. Stress is part of the human experience. By centering ourselves and having a strong mind we may not be able to control events, but we can control our responses to events. As life challenges come your way, you now have a strong resource to take in the stress, evaluate and release it from your body. Stress is the number one cause of illness and anything that allows the stress to flow into and out of your life and body is worth more than a store full of vitamins.

Be gentle with yourself and have patience… awareness comes in stages. This is the type of book to review from time to time. Discover a concept introduced in these pages that interests you and learn more. As you practice and heal, you will grow and understand more with each meditation and review of this material.

Time does not heal all wounds. Wounds become part of you and will continue to impact your emotions and behaviors. With self-awareness the wounds become something to love and appreciate about yourself and have more positive impact than negative impact. Meditation, going inward, loving yourself, knowing yourself, accepting yourself, caring for yourself, and maintaining presence and clarity heals wounds.

Signs you are making progress:

You feel comfortable with yourself.

You like yourself.

You are starting to set boundaries easily.

You are kinder to yourself when you make a mistake.

You acknowledge mistakes with grace and confidence.

You are kinder to others when they make mistakes.

You prioritize time for yourself.

You take time to collect your thoughts before responding to those that trigger you.

You can detach from those who are not good for you.

You feel like today is a good today.

You feel like this moment is a happy moment.

You trust that good things are in your future.

Your ability to heal is greater than anyone has ever led you to believe.

About the Author

This author arrived at an amazing point in life and from this point, created a manual to help herself and others. At this point I lost my career, marriage, money, health in one short swift stroke. From this point I focused on myself, meditation, love, gratitude. Lost, crying, confused became a gift for finding joy, clarity. I never gave up, well, I did sometimes, but then screwed up my energy and started again….and again…and again.

I, Dr. Sydnie Bryant, AP, draw from 30 years of natural health care worker experience in massage, energy work, Chinese Medicine, spiritual growth, and development.

I am thankful for all the teachers who came before me. This information is ancient wisdom repeatedly accessed from angels and guides and reworded for new ears to hear.

I am thankful for my amazing family and friends who stood by me through all of this.

I would be amazingly happy if one person finds this information helpful in their journey out of darkness or overwhelming stress.

I would be amazingly happy if one person finds this information useful when they have a happy life but use these words to take it to a new level of presence and spirit.

I am amazingly happy.

For one-on-one sessions, go to
bryantwellnesscenter.com.

www.ingramcontent.com/pod-product-compliance
Lightning Source LLC
Chambersburg PA
CBHW071431130726
47997CB00006B/2035